THREE CAPITALS FOR TWO STATES

THREE CAPITALS FOR TWO STATES

Analysis of Jerusalem's Sovereignty and Perspectives

A Monograph
by
MAJ Carl Dick
US Army

MENS EST CLAVIS VICTORIA

School of Advanced Military Studies United States Army
Command and General Staff College Fort Leavenworth, Kansas

To order additional copies of this book, contact:
Xlibris Corporation
1-888-795-4274
www.Xlibris.com
Orders@Xlibris.com
102656

This book is dedicated to all Sappers who choose to enter the breach; To my wife Shawn for the love and support she provides, and to Dr. Alice Butler-Smith for facilitating my opportunity to choose a subject others might want to read.

CONTENTS

SCHOOL OF ADVANCED MILITARY STUDIES

MONOGRAPH APPROVAL

MAJ Carl Dick

Title of Monograph: Three Capitals for Two States: Analysis of Jerusalem's Sovereignty and Perspectives

Approved by:

_____ Monograph Director
Dr. Alice Butler-Smith, PhD

_____ Second Reader
Peter Fischer, COL, GE Army

_____ Director,
Wayne W. Grigsby Jr., COL, IN   School of Advanced
                                  Military Studies

_____ Director,
Robert F. Baumann, PhD   Graduate Degree Programs

ABSTRACT

THREE CAPITALS FOR TWO STATES: ANALYSIS OF JERUSALEM'S SOVEREIGNTY AND PERSPECTIVES by MAJ Carl Dick, US Army, 56 pages.

This study argues that there are historical reasons to focus on Jerusalem first and to use an international Holy Basin methodology to bring Israel and the Palestinian National Authority together toward a workable compromise. This analysis identifies the strategic compromises required to create two distinct capital zones that grants sovereignty and legitimacy over respective capitals for the state of Israel and a future state of Palestine. To address the Arab-Israeli conflict, there have been numerous Middle East peace processes, two intifadas, and six US administrations with little demonstrated progress. In terms of religion and national identity, Jerusalem is a central factor for both Israelis and Palestinians, to the people of three world religions, and to the international community.

The critical factors to achieve compromise are sovereignty over their respective capitals combined with international recognition and possible control over remaining contested holy places. Resolving the city's role as a national capital for two states can lead to resolving other critical Arab-Israeli issues. The international community has perpetuated the conflict by withholding Jerusalem sovereignty from Israel and the Arab population. When Britain ended their Palestine mandate in 1948, the UN failed to deliberately enforce their vision of a separate Jerusalem entity, or corpus separatum. The UN continued to withhold sovereignty while the city was divided for nineteen years between Jordan and Israel and when the city was reunited in 1967. The lack of an international mandate for sixty-four years while fighting for utopian concepts has perpetuated the conflict by delaying the self-determination of the Palestinian population and withholding sovereignty over Israel's declared capital. Peace negotiations must recognize and incorporate the interests of both sides, but until each side is ready to strictly divide the Old City, an international Holy Basin zone has the potential to create a new reality while moving incrementally from confrontation to cooperation.

INTRODUCTION

Jerusalem can become a beacon for all the nations of the world, and they will walk about in its light. It is our duty to construct this beacon. It is our duty to set a light in it. This is a great and difficult historical responsibility.[1]

—Jerusalem Deputy Mayor Rabbi Cohen, 1967

The Middle East peace process has been a continuous open-ended problem and the focus of United States and international diplomatic effort for the last sixty years. As the focal point of three of the world's monotheistic religions, Jerusalem is one of the most divisive and complex issues in our time. It is vitally important to Jewish, Christian, and Muslim people throughout the world. Unfortunately, Jerusalem is either so overwhelming to understand or left as the last issue for discussion during diplomatic negotiations between Israelis and Palestinians. An analysis of the current two-state solution realistically scaled down to a two-capital solution creates a need to understand how important Jerusalem is in the broader process toward peace.

In terms of ethnicity, Jerusalem can be defined as two distinct cities, with Israeli Jews and Palestinian Arabs, yet they have overlapping geographic zones and demographics. It would be easy to take a map and divide the city into two respective blocks representing each side's interests, but that would require ignoring history, religion, and critical holy places that are important to two or more groups. There is no other city with more complexity. As the United Nations was created, the early push for an international Jerusalem concept was an attempt by the world powers to incorporate the interests of Christians as well as break the impasse between two vastly different Arab and Jewish

---

[1] Michael Dumper, *The Politics of Jerusalem Since 1967* (New York: Columbia University Press, 1997), 10.

viewpoints. Past negotiations have either ignored Jerusalem's religious nature or focused solely on religious sites while ignoring the political perspectives of each side.

To understand past peace process breakdowns, the United Nations first failed to implement an international Jerusalem, then withheld sovereignty over Jerusalem, and starting in 1967, failed to include thirty years of an international zone methodology that ensures access to all parties. Unfortunately, all resolutions since then were continuations of the decisive and polarized 1967 agreement, United Nations Security Council Resolution 242, demanding a withdrawal to prewar borders after the Six-Day War. The critical factors to achieve compromise over Jerusalem are sovereignty over their respective capitals, combined with international recognition of the two capitals and possible control over remaining contested holy places. This study argues that there are historical reasons to focus on Jerusalem first and identifies the strategic compromises required to create two distinct capital zones that grants sovereignty and legitimacy over respective capitals for the state of Israel and a future state of Palestine. Finally, an international Holy Basin methodology has the potential to bring Israel and the Palestinian National Authority together toward a workable compromise.

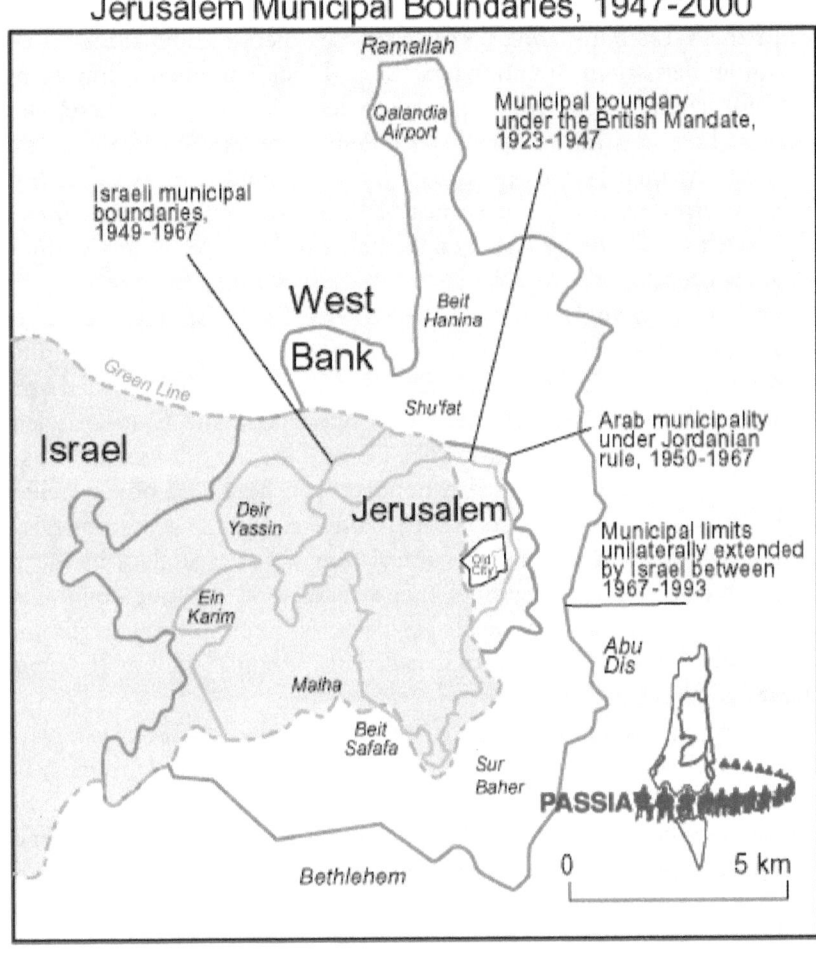

Jerusalem Municipal Boundaries, 1947-2000

The Palestinian Academic Society for the Study of International Affairs

(PASSIA)

Figure 1. Jerusalem boundary changes through time. Reproduced with permission from the publisher of *Jerusalem Municipal Boundaries: 1947-2000* (Jerusalem: The Palestinian Academic Society for the Study of International Affairs, 2010).

Israelis and Palestinians have trouble scaling down their distinct national requirements, with defined and secured borders, on to Jerusalem as a future capital for their respective nations. Regarding issues such as settlements, right of return, and refugees, Palestinians focus on Gaza and the West Bank as the future state of Palestine with defined borders but contradict these demands with utopian goals for an open and undivided Jerusalem. These same issues in the West Bank are easier to analyze when isolated from historical and religious Jerusalem. Solutions to these difficult problems, however, are increasingly complicated when applied to Jerusalem and are therefore not universal. There is a Jewish/Israeli Jerusalem incorporating West Jerusalem and Israeli settlements or towns in East Jerusalem, and there is a Palestinian/Arab Jerusalem that incorporates most of East Jerusalem. Exact terminology will be used to deconstruct how two capitals can live side by side within the two-state concept.

Israel has grudgingly accepted the two-state solution and focuses on a land-for-peace swap that will adjust the West Bank borders but still fights for sovereignty rights over a united Jerusalem and ignores the fight for Palestinian self-determination in East Jerusalem. Palestinians demand East Jerusalem as their capital, based on the 1949 armistice Green Line, yet grudgingly recognize that Israel has interests over Jewish population centers and on key religious areas that reside east of the Green Line. While recognizing that Israelis and Palestinians have each demanded control over all of Jerusalem in the past, neither side can achieve everything they would want. To scale down further into Jerusalem, all Arab and Israeli perspectives, interests, and requirements revolve around one critical location called the Temple Mount in Israel or al-Haram al-Sharif in Arabic.

Lord Hugh Caradon, diplomatic author of the 1967 United Nations Resolution 242, wrote a monograph for the National Defense University titled *The Future of Jerusalem: A Review of Proposals for the Future of the City*.[2] Since then there have been many Middle East peace processes, two intifadas, and six US administrations with little demonstrated progress. Jerusalem has either been considered too complex to solve or has been the last item during negotiation talks. All Arab-Israeli final status issues, however, relate to Jerusalem, making it the key to any future Palestinian-Israeli peace negotiation. What does Jerusalem represent to each stakeholder and to future peace negotiations? Does an international zone or a Holy Basin methodology, which protects only those contested religious areas of Jerusalem, bridge differences of trust and acceptance?

Answers to these questions above are broken down into four sections. They outline four negotiating strategies to include respecting the legitimate perspectives of each side, sovereignty over a capital city, scaling down to understand the requirements for two capitals, and international legitimacy over

---

[2]   Hugh Caradon, *The Future of Jerusalem: A Review of Proposals for the Future of the City* (Washington, DC: National Defense University, 1979), 1.

areas that may forever remain contested. The first section of the monograph asserts that the city of Jerusalem is the key to future peace between Israelis and Palestinians based on internal and external legitimacy rights as nation-states. Influence over Jerusalem is important to the peace process based on key holy sites that provide a religious, historical, and national identity for Jews, Arabs, and Christians throughout the world. Identifying their interests and differences over holy places as well as sovereignty over their respective populations in the city will indicate overlapping tension and opportunities.

Secondly, sovereignty and legitimacy will be defined through the examination of Jerusalem's role during Arab-Israeli state-building exercises from the 1920s through 1967. Today's two-state concept was suggested and debated as early as 1937 and 1947 though rejected by Arab nations. From the desire to protect key Christian holy places by world powers, the separation of Jerusalem from Arab or Jewish control was central to all other discussions. Today's utopian concepts such as "open city," "corpus separatum," "undivided," and "demilitarized" have been carried over from pre-1948 negotiations, from Jerusalem's nineteen-year division and diplomacy following the 1967 Six-Day War.

The third section reviews the taxonomy of Jerusalem strategies within the peaces process starting in 1993 in order to understand if there were similar operational concepts for the city of Jerusalem that may bridge differences. Finally, a focus on an international Holy Basin zone methodology that can bridge overlapping interests will be examined. If the goals of protection and access for the holy places can be united with the need to ensure sovereignty over two nation's capitals, then the question is where to place the capital and, ultimately, national boundaries. The two-state solution must be deconstructed to understand what two capitals within Jerusalem would require. Currently, Jerusalem has a predominately Jewish zone and a Palestinian zone; however, they do not follow an easy East/West division along the old 1949 armistice boundaries. The monograph will conclude with a general outlook for 2011 as the Palestinian National Authority nears its two-year self-imposed deadline to create a Palestinian state.

Even though Jerusalem contains many of the final status issues that affect Arab-Israeli peace negotiations, this paper will not address the issues of Palestinian refugees, right of return, Gaza, the Golan Heights, or the composition of the West Bank because these issues cannot be solved without a political solution dividing Jerusalem. This monograph focuses on what Jerusalem represents to Israel, to Palestinians, and to the international community in the context of a final peace settlement. Many Jerusalem studies are broken down into three types: those that define a religious importance, those that delve into detailed land planning, and finally those that are political or legalistic. This paper will focus on the latter and uses an interest-based approach as a way to group Jerusalem's complex issues. In the *Cooperation and Conflict Journal* addressing an approach to complex problems, Cecilia Albin "proposed that intractable conflicts such as that over Jerusalem are best approached by using a combination of the strategies to tackle the typically core problem of sovereignty."[3] Simply, one negotiating concept will not bridge every demand, and complex problems will require a complex set of strategies.

The literature review includes international peace agreements reaching back to the Ottoman status quo environment in 1913, the rise of both Jewish and Arab nationalism, the British Mandate period from 1918 to 1948, and to the early UN resolutions that attempted to keep Jerusalem separate from any non-Christian nation. Critical primary sources will be US and UN reports from past peace processes and policy statements by key participants including Israeli and Palestinian leaders. This understanding helps to develop a comprehensive approach to identify feasible, acceptable, and suitable solutions that create two capitals in Jerusalem. Operational frameworks analyzed include 1993 Oslo agreements, the 2000-2001 Taba Negotiations, and the Palestinian Authority's two-year statehood plan. Though it is difficult to read material on Jerusalem that remains understandingly biased toward one side, research from both Arab and Israeli institutions and think tanks were used to understand the perspectives of both Palestinians and Israelis. Research examples include reports from the Jerusalem Institute for Israeli Studies (JIIS), Institute for National Security Studies (INSS), and the Institute for Palestine Studies and the Israeli-Palestinian Center for Research Institute. The author's four previous trips to Israel provided an understanding on Israeli narratives, and attendance at an American Task Force on Palestine gala in Washington, DC, improved the author's understanding on the Palestinian narrative. Finally, the author used a grant from the United States Air Force Institute for National Security Studies to walk the ground in both West and East Jerusalem in order to conduct personal interviews and to understand the consequences of a divided city.

---

[3]   Cecilia Albin, "On the Future of Jerusalem," *Cooperation and Conflict Journal 32* (March 1997), 29-77.

Jerusalem Is the Key to Future Negotiations

The following section describes fundamental Israeli and Palestinian interests as well as tensions among many stakeholders in Jerusalem in order to provide an understanding of the importance of Jerusalem within the Arab-Israeli peace process. Jerusalem resides in the Levant, and four factors will be analyzed to understand Jerusalem's importance and analysis of this complex environment. These include the three religious groups and key holy places, the rise of Arab/Palestinian and Jewish nationalism, and the international community's altered view of Jerusalem as a world capital.

The Importance of Jerusalem Defined by Religious Identity

Jerusalem has an ancient history and, as a result, fits differently within a host of competing narratives. The honorable Evan Wilson, the United States consulate general during the 1967 war, deftly summarized the central plot in each of them when he described Jerusalem as "a Dome, A Tomb and a Wall; a Crescent, a Cross and a Star; three faiths, three worlds, three ways of life."[4] The Arab-Israeli problems could be solved rationally if religion was removed from the discussion; however, religion could never be removed from the historical environment. The three monotheistic religions of Judaism, Christianity, and Islam all derive historical and religious importance from key places within Jerusalem. While the infighting and hatred seem to sustain the conflict between West and East, these three religions have some commonalities that

---

4   Evan M. Wilson, *Jerusalem, Key to Peace* (Washington, DC: The Middle East Institute, 1970), 1.

are historical and cultural. Both Christianity and Islam accept the Judean Old Testament, with Christianity believing in a prophet who preached in the Old City around 30 CE and an Islamic prophet who taught in 570 CE. Specific holy places that are sacred to the three religions all revolve inside Jerusalem's Old City, specifically the Temple Mount or al-Haram al-Sharif.

Judaism is based on Abraham's lineage, history, and geography. King David conquered the land of Palestine and united the twelve Israeli tribes, integrating religious and political power as he moved his capital to the religious center of Canaan or Levant, a small town called Jerusalem.[5] David's son Solomon built the First Temple, which survived until Babylon's destruction in 587 BCE. To understand the Jewish narrative, it is essential to know that their self-determination and identity is based on the Jew's first exile to Babylon and after 67 CE, a second exile lasting almost twenty centuries. From the time of Abraham until Rome's destruction of the Second Temple, Judaism was "temple-based," meaning Jerusalem-based.

Palestine—or the area encompassing present-day Israel, Lebanon, Jordan, and parts of Syria—was at the crossroads of the Persian, Egyptian, and Assyrian empires; and Jerusalem was on the central mountain route that linked Beersheba and Bethlehem in the south with Ramallah and Jenin to the north.[6] "In the second half of the eighth century B.C.E. the built-up area of Jerusalem expanded from the City of David to the western Mount Zion hill and the city reached its maximal size in biblical times . . . dozens of settlements of all size ranks from regional towns to small villages and tiny farmsteads—appeared in the hill country of Judah to the south of Jerusalem."[7] A water source was the reason the City of David was built on a smaller hill surrounded by larger hills—to include Mount Scopus, Mount of Olives, and other larger hills—and a few miles away from the main road network. Aside from rainwater-collecting cisterns, the Gihon Spring at the base of the hill in the Kidron Valley provided the only nearby water source. The City of David is not within the current Old City walls but remains as ruins immediately south of the Old City's Dung Gate and as archeological foundations under the Palestinian town of Silwan. The current Temple Mount complex was built over two mountain tops, with the smaller one used for David's administration and the tallest one for religious structures. To the east of the Old City on both sides of Kidron Valley are many

---

[5] Meir Ben-Dov, *Carta's Illustrated History of Jerusalem*, 2nd ed. (Jerusalem: Karta, 2006).

[6] Ibid., 7.

[7] Andrew G. Vaughn and Ann E. Killebrew, *Jerusalem in Bible and Archaeology: the First Temple Period* (Atlanta: The Society of Biblical Literature, 2003), 82.

gravesites considered holy places for both Jews and Arabs during past peace negotiations.

Israelis of today cannot be thought of as having one narrative. Thomas Friedman identified at least five groups: secular Jews, religious Orthodox, settlement Zionists, Ultraorthodox, and finally the Diaspora throughout the world.[8] The dichotomies between national Zionists and religious Jews have complicated their viewpoints on the state of Israel and on Jerusalem as the source of their identity. David Ben-Gurion, the first Israeli prime minister, however, did not view the gulf between Israelis and the Jewish Diaspora as vast. "There is no Jewish community in the world which lives with such a deep feeling of unity and identification with the totality of Jews in the world as does the Jewish community in [Israel]."[9] Split between the four groups has been hundreds of thousands of Eastern European, American, and African Jewish immigrants, complicating any attempt to identify common tensions and interests.

The word *Jerusalem* may not be in the Koran, but Muslims and Arab Palestinians derive religious importance from Jerusalem. Muslims first prayed toward "Jerusalem [as] the first of the two *qiblas*, and the third (after Mecca and Medina) of the most sacred lands."[10] The Omayyad Dynasty built the Al Quds Mosque in 691 CE on the site of Abraham's sacrificial rock, the Temple Mount, hundreds of miles from Mecca and less than seventy years after Mohammed's death. Without a historical basis for state nationalism, Palestinian leaders derive their legitimacy from the Arab diaspora. Palestinian president Abbas has stated that he will put up any agreement to a populist referendum because "any arrangement for the future of Jerusalem (and especially one for the Old City and the surroundings) and the holy sites will require the approval of the important Arab and Muslim states such as Saudi Arabia, Egypt, Jordan, Morocco, and others."[11]

Not forgetting the third monotheistic religion, Christianity focuses on Jesus and his life in Jerusalem's holy lands. Born in Bethlehem, which now lies in the West Bank south of the Jerusalem municipality, Jesus preached

---

[8] Thomas Friedman, *From Beirut to Jerusalem* (New York: Farrar, Straus and Giroux: 1990), 155.

[9] Avraham Avi-hai, Ben-Gurion, *State-Builder: Principles and Pragmatism* (New York: Keter Publishing House, 1974), 105.

[10] Charles D. Matthews, "A Muslim Iconoclast on the Merits of Jerusalem and Palestine," *Journal of the American Oriental Society* 56 (March 1936), 1.

[11] Yitzhak Reiter, *Options for the Administration of the Holy Places in the Old City of Jerusalem* (Jerusalem: Jerusalem Institute for Israeli Studies, 2008), 2.

in many Jerusalem areas including the Temple Mount. The Church of the Holy Sepulcher marks his crucifixion by Pontius Pilate on the hill called Calvary. The Via Dolorosa commemorates the last journey Jesus made through Jerusalem, which starts in the current Muslim quarter and ends at the Church of the Holy Sepulcher. It is impossible to see the landscape of a Calvary hilltop where Jesus was crucified by viewing the relatively flat Old City streets without understanding that the valley between the City of David and Calvary has been filled by centuries of growth, debris, and change. Due to rival Christian philosophies and the competition between Eastern Orthodox and Western churches, Sultan Osman III in 1757 created rules to protect both specific sites and religious access called the Status Quo.[12] These two-century-old rules are reflected and codified in treaties to include the 1922 League of Nations Charter and the UN Partition Plan of 1947. Today, there are many Christian groups—including Armenians, Russian Orthodox, Ethiopians, Mormons, and Protestants—protecting and ensuring access to hundreds of churches in the region, and they adapt contemporary reality to past Status Quo rules.

Key Holy Places Provide Internal Legitimacy

Israeli and Palestinian identities cannot be separated from specific holy places, with holy books and stories describing historic religious events. The focus, importance, and reasons for specific sites were used as evidence during past negotiations to fight for respective negotiating positions. Marshall Breger, Yitzhak Reiter, and Leonard Hammer compiled reports on key holy sites for the Routledge Studies in Middle Eastern Politics titled *Holy Places in the Israeli-Palestinian Conflict*.[13] These key holy places in and around Jerusalem are the underlying differences in "confrontation and co-existence" that occurred before and after Israel's independence. Four areas that have Jewish and Muslim overlaps include Mount Scopus, the Mount of Olives, the Old City, and specifically the Temple Mount, or al-Haram al-Sharif in Arabic. These articles highlight that the Arab waqf and religion in general always trump politics. The Routledge researchers used specific places to identify historical and realistic status-quo measures that provide a working coexistence model.

---

[12] Ibid. "The Ottoman Status Quo edicts by the sultan in 1852 and 1853 relates to the seven Christian holy sites in Jerusalem and Bethlehem, of which only two are in the Old City."

[13] Marshall Breger, Yitzhak Reiter, and Leonard Hammer, *Holy Places in the Israeli-Palestinian Conflict* (New York: Routledge, 2010), 1.

The religious places overlap on the most holy shrines in Jerusalem, the Temple Mount or al-Haram al-Sharif and the Western Wall. "The Western Wall (or Wailing) Wall is part of the retaining wall built in 20 B.C.E. under the direction of King Herod to support the massive structures of the Temple Mount above."[14] The Western Wall is not simply a religious site for Judaism. Muslims often cite three reasons to claim the Western Wall as a Muslim religious site, possibly to discredit Jewish influence. Some believe that the prophet Mohammed tied his horse, Burqa, to a site at the Western Wall during the final night journey. The destruction of the Maghrabi quarter in order to restore the Western Wall plaza and Britain's mandated holy places list cited the Western Wall as a Muslim waqf are two addition reasons Israelis fear that if the Old City and the Temple Mount were retained in the Palestinian capital of East Jerusalem, they would lose access to their two most important religious places.

Included in past peace talks have been holy place access, legality, protection, and shared importance. Where to divide Jerusalem comes down to a choice as to which holy places are vital by two or more stakeholders. Mount Scopus was specified as Jewish land in the 1949 Armistice Agreements. UN resolutions continued the partition plan's goals of religious protection and access. UN resolution 50, issued on 29 May 1948, "urges all governments and authorities concerned to take every possible precaution for the protection of the Holy Places and the City of Jerusalem, including access to all shrines and sanctuaries for the purpose of worship by those who have an established right to visit and worship at them."[15]

Arabs that demand access to Muslim sites must remember that Jews were denied access to the Western Wall for Jordan's nineteen-year West Bank occupation. Currently, access to the Temple Mount is open for Christians in the mornings and for Muslims in the afternoon. Jews are advised not to visit the Temple Mount, both for religious reasons (not to inadvertently step were the Temple called the Holy of Holies once stood) and to prevent conflict with the Arabs.

Asking if Jerusalem and key holy sites are negotiable, Segal found that "most Palestinians would seriously consider a proposal in which West Jerusalem would be under Israeli sovereignty and East Jerusalem would be under Palestinian sovereignty, with a special arrangement for Israeli control

---

14   Chad F. Emmett, "The Status Quo Solution for Jerusalem," *Journal of Palestinian Studies 26* (Winter, 1997): 16-28.

15   United Nations Security Council Resolution 50, accessed 14 March 2011, http://un.org/documents/sc/res/1948/scres48.htm/.

of the Jewish neighborhoods in East Jerusalem. The Old City would be dealt with separately."[16] In terms of levels or changes in scale, both sides have detailed requirements for their respective nation-state, but they have idealistic concepts for their capital and respective holy site.

Current international agreements focus on four holy place issues: identity classification, legal/historical, protection, and access. Protection for the international community's three religions has been discussed in the 2001 Mitchell Report and the 2002 US Human Rights Report. There are Christian holy sites in the latest 1993 Vatican-Israel Fundamental Agreement.

Self-Determination and the Rise of Arab and Zionist Nationalism

To understand how national identities and historical meanings are created, Charles Hill in Grand Strategies uses literature, interactions, and wars to describe "such matters as how a people begin to identity itself as a nation."[17] At the same time that Lieutenant T. E. Lawrence was stirring up Arab nationalism, Jewish or Zionist nationalism arose both inside and outside of Palestine. Theodor Herzl stirred up Jewish nationalism with his publication, *The Jewish State*, and his subsequent visit to Palestine in 1898. David Ben-Gurion sought out accommodations during the British Mandate period to create an Israeli State through the early Jewish Agency. While agreeing to the UN Partition Plan in General Agreement 181, Ben-Gurion settled for a state that did not include Jerusalem. The Jewish Agency fought for statehood, sovereignty, and legitimacy while the Arab nations fought to destroy Jewish interests in Palestine.

Self-determination plays a key part in any conflict with a minority attempting to fight for recognition, freedom, or power. World examples include South Africans, Northern Ireland, and even African Americans in the United States. Jews were persecuted for centuries and fought to have a land of their own. Judaism's last daily prayer, "Next year in Jerusalem," is now being used by Palestinians as a satirical and an emotional statement for a future state.[18] The Palestinian narrative has its own fears and hopes. Islamic organizations

---

16   Jeremy Segal, *Negotiating Jerusalem* (Albany: State University of New York Press, 2000), viii. The University of Maryland's Jerusalem Project questioned over 1,500 Israeli Jews and some 870 Palestinians in order to understand Jerusalem in the eyes of each side's perspectives and opinions.

17   Charles Hill, *Grand Strategies* (New Haven: Yale University Press, 2010), 7.

18   Comedian Maysoon Zayid performing in Washington, DC, for the American Task Force for Palestine Fifth Annual Gala, 20 October 2010.

use religious documents and historical references to postulate the importance of Jerusalem to Muslims and especially to Palestinians. Palestinians are broken down into four subgroups. First, there are 1.7 million Palestinians in the West Bank, Gaza, and East Jerusalem; and then there are those living in refugee camps in Jordan, Syria, and Lebanon.[19] The other two categories are Palestinians broken down to Christian and Muslim Palestinians, with the latter including varying ideologies from moderate Fatah and extremist groups led by Hamas. Two related groups are Israeli Arabs and Muslims throughout the world. Palestinians, according to *New York Times* journalist Thomas Friedman, have learned to fight on their own, with little Arab League financial support. There are many Palestinian narratives, but a common experience has been derived through the British Mandate period and refugee status over the last sixty years.[20]

Three adapting Christian tendencies have improved the chances for Palestinians to achieve their own state. The first is due to the need to protect the Christian Arab community, the second to support Palestinian's self-determination, and the third is recognition that most of the holy places remained east of the 1967 Green Line. However, Palestinian leadership is using religion to sway politics. The 2009 Kairos Palestine Document, published by Palestinian Christians and Jerusalem religious leaders, assert that there must not be a (Jewish) nation built on religion, ignoring twenty-two Arab states with Islamic state religion, and uses delegitimization to propose that Israelis have no historical ties to Jerusalem.[21] Religious interests are intertwined with political interests, and documents such as this deny Israeli self-determination in order to defend self-determination rights of Palestinians.

Jerusalem's Shifting Importance as a World Capital

While the peace process has been an incremental progression, the environment in and around Jerusalem continued to change due to war, peace, and internal conflict. Three changes through recent history will be analyzed. These include a powerful Christian influence, incremental peace agreements, and a focus to East Jerusalem as a future Palestinian capital. Early Christian nations' focus on Christian holy places was an important factor while Arab and

---

19   Friedman, *From Beirut to Jerusalem*, 386.
20   Rashid Khalidi, *Palestinian Identity: The Construction of Modern National Consciousness* (New York: Columbia University Press, 1997), 195.
21   Kairos Document, *A Moment of Truth*, http://www.kairospalestine.ps, December 2009.

Jewish nationalism was debated after World War II. "The fate of Jerusalem and the other Holy Places in Palestine, so strongly linked with the origins of Christianity, has always commanded the Holy See's interests and has led it on a number of occasions to undertake political initiatives designed to guarantee a Catholic presence in the Holy Land."[22] While not supporting either an Arab state, a Jewish state, or two states partitioned, "the best solution to protect the Catholic Church's rights in Palestine would be the internationalization of Jerusalem."[23] Since the British ended the mandate, trust for the Christian holy places has been in the hands of both Israeli and Jordanian/Palestinian Christians. Understanding that Yasser Arafat did cater to Palestinian Christians helps understand the low-level influence or intrigue from the Vatican and American Christians during the rise of the PLO. Declining Christian viewpoints may have decreased their importance, but the Jerusalem problem remains complex.

The second factor is the incremental changes that each negotiation through war and peace forces on Jerusalem as a system. Every stakeholder reacts to the new realities, and the world would not be where it is without adapting and adjusting to every circumstance. Peace agreements as well as the intifadas, the rise of Hamas, and wars in Lebanon and Gaza have helped everyone understand the complexity surrounding Jerusalem. Although Jerusalem and the Palestinian cause were heavily debated, Jerusalem was not in the final 1979 Camp David Accords that ended peace negotiations between Egypt and Israel. The city is vitally important to each side but was deemed too complicated to be negotiated over Sinai. Peace between Israel and Jordan did not solve Jerusalem; however, these incremental agreements helped pave the way to today's two-state discussions.

Finally, as the world shifts toward preparing for a Palestinian state, the focus turns on East Jerusalem. For the American Task Force for Palestine (ATFP) Fifth Annual Gala, President Mahmoud Abbas highlighted "our right to self-determination . . . and the establishment of the state of Palestine, with East Jerusalem as its capital, living side by side with the state of Israel."[24] "Within Israel, Jerusalem is viewed as the third rail of Israeli Politics. To date, no major political party has proposed sharing sovereignty with the Palestinians.

---

[22] Silvio Ferrari, "The Holy See and the Postwar Palestine Issue: The Internationalization of Jerusalem and the Protection of the Holy Places," *International Affairs*, 261.

[23] Ibid.

[24] Mahmoud Abbas, "Letter to Dr. Ziad Asali," Palestine National Authority, 13 October 2010.

Yet, among Palestinians, some 94% say that even if it was the only way that a Palestinian state could come into being, they would not accept Israeli's claim that it allows sovereign over all of Jerusalem."[25] The next section describes the critical role Jerusalem provides as a capital for two states, including sovereign and legitimate authority.

---

[25]   Segal, *Negotiating Jerusalem*, vii.

SOVEREIGNTY AND LEGITIMACY OVER JERUSALEM

No world body would attempt to separate Washington, DC, from the United States or Paris from France. Yet these two analogies help readers understand Jerusalem as a nation's capital in terms of state sovereignty. Sovereignty has internal and external characteristics brought about from the 1648 Westphalia agreements, which stressed international relations and how state systems "agreed to conduct their official interactions."[26] Sovereignty and state power were defined by Max Weber as "the right of final decision" or "a state is a human community that successfully claims the monopoly of the legitimate use of physical force within a given territory."[27] External legitimacy is granted by the international community, usually through the United Nations (UN), whereas internal legitimacy is granted by a nation's population through elections, general support, or polling data. The Palestinian National Authority (PNA) or Palestinian Authority (PA) is used to define the government entity created during the 1993 Oslo Peace Accords and was accorded levels of external sovereignty over lands within the West Bank and East Jerusalem. This section will describe how the international community withheld legitimacy of Jerusalem as a declared capital for the state of Israel. Regarding a future state of Palestine, a political framework that creates two capitals for both Israel and for the Palestinian National Authority can help resolve remaining issues such as refuges, right of return, and settlements within the West Bank.

---

[26] Hill, *Grand Strategies*, 4.

[27] Max Weber, *Politics as a Vocation*, eds. H. H. Gerth and C. Wright Mils (New York: Oxford University Press, 1958), 78.

The Green Line refers back to the dividing line that existed between Jordan and Israel, before 5 June 1967; however, this line was the resulting armistice border agreed to during the 1949 United Nations-sponsored peace talks. The armistice line created a nineteen-year split between an Israeli West Jerusalem and a Jordanian East Jerusalem. West and East Jerusalem will be defined in this paper based on the Green Line. Arab East Jerusalem will be used to define the majority Arab population zones, minus the ten to twelve Israeli towns within East Jerusalem built after 1967. The Old City and the most critical holy places important to all three religions reside east of the Green Line in East Jerusalem.

Jerusalem as a capital for two population groups can only be explained by the history of the land. The story of Jerusalem must be told through the lens of increased nationalism and self-determination caused by the disillusionment of the Ottoman Empire after World War I. Then after World War II, the world community, through the newly formed United Nations, attempted to find an equitable solution to this conflict. Finally after Jerusalem was divided for nineteen years, the Six-Day War drastically changed the narrative of Jerusalem's populations and brought the Palestinian cause to the forefront. Three concepts will be examined to explain how the Israeli-Palestinian confrontation developed, the withdrawal of a foreign "mandate" country in 1948, the death of a separate international Jerusalem concept from 1947 to 1949, and the refusal to negotiate Jerusalem sovereignty after the city was united in 1967.

International Legitimacy through an External Mandate: 1918-1948

As mentioned in the first section, the League of Nations attempted to replace the Great Power's drive for colonial annexation with a temporary and internationally recognized mandate granted to Britain. A land, whose population or leaders are not prepared to lead or is contested by multiple groups, had in the past required foreign external management. This terminology may be similar to colonialism; however, the European powers were not yet willing to leave their colonies and historical ties to past empires. Lands previously controlled by World War I opponents became the newest nation-states.[28]

---

[28]   The Council on the League of Nations, 24 July 1922, http://mideastweb.org. In the League of Nations Charter, the remnants from Turkey were listed as A mandates and included Palestine, Mesopotamia, Syria, and Lebanon. B mandates focused on Central African nations, and C mandates were German colonies in the Pacific.

The 1916 Balfour document, though never approved by the British Parliament, was not the only document granting future protection of Jews. It took on a more powerful form when the Palestine Mandate became a stand-alone section in article 22 of the Covenant of the League of Nations. The Lausanne Conference of 1922-1923, which finally abolished the Ottoman Empire and ended the war with the new government of Turkey, granted Britain the mandate over Palestine. The 1919 Covenant of the League of Nations Charter recognized both the Balfour Declaration as well as the Sykes-Picot Agreement. This was followed up with the 3 December 1924 American-British mandate convention protecting economic interests.

While the mandate details were debated from 1918 to 1922, the populations within Palestine struggled for four years under military administration. British diplomat Lord Balfour, recognizing that legitimacy and speed were essential and even suggesting that the United States should be the mandate country, wrote to the US secretary of state that a mandate government "must seem secure in the eyes of the populations concerned. Without this it cannot possess the necessary prestige, or exercise the necessary influence."[29]

Since the holy places were in contention between the three religions, a subarticle protected both access and freedom of worship. Article 9 tasked the mandate government to safeguard religious administrations including waqfs and the Status Quo religious rules. Article 13 focused on four goals for the holy places: "Preserving existing rights, of securing free access to the Holy Places, religious buildings or sites and the free exercise of worship, while ensuring the requirements of public order and decorum." Article 14, recognizing the complex nature of religious Jerusalem, outlines the requirements for a special commission to regulate religious administrations, and article 15 reiterated "free exercise of all forms of worship .... No discrimination of any kind shall be made between the inhabitants of Palestine on the ground of race, religion or language. No person shall be excluded from Palestine on the sole ground of his religious belief."[30]

As complex as Palestine was after a world war with multiple stakeholders, the central idea remained that religion always trumped politics. The concept of a mandate grants an internationally recognized power with temporary authority for natural nation-state activities such as foreign relations, embassies, treaties, citizenships, and protecting the populations. When Clement Attlee declared in 1947 that Britain was broke and informed the new United Nations

---

[29] Lord Balfour to the US secretary of state, Washington, DC, 24 July 1922 in *The Palestine Mandate* (Salisbury, NC: The Division of Near Eastern Affairs, 1977), 58.

[30] The Palestine Mandate, (Salisbury, NC: US Department of State Division of Near Eastern Affairs, 1977), 15.

that Britain would end their mandate responsibilities in Palestine (as well as leave their prime jewel India), the world was forced to debate Jerusalem's sovereignty, expectantly raising Jewish and Arab nationalistic expectations. The next section scales down into the mandate concept in Palestine to the level of Jerusalem as a future capital for two states.

Post-WWII: Jerusalem Sovereignty Withheld from the Realities of War

In the movie *O Jerusalem*, the story of Said, a Palestinian working in America, and Bobby, a Jewish American soldier, describes Jews and Arabs surviving World War II. They struggle to contemplate Britain departing from Jerusalem with the creation of a Jewish state side by side with an Arab state.[31]

There are four historical reasons why the international Jerusalem concept was fought for. The first was the large mass of thirty-plus religious holy places, which no one country could control. Second, there were many nation-states protecting Christian interests. Sykes-Picot was the 1916 agreement that cut up Ottoman Empire lands to three Christian-based countries. Russians wanted to protect Orthodox Christian sites and their historical ties dating back to the 1800s, the French protected Catholic interests, and the British protected Protestant-based churches.[32] The third aspect reflected the demographic shifts and rising self-determination of both Arabs and Jews. British promises to the Hussein family during World War I contradicted promises to Jewish nationalists through the Balfour Agreement, which caused a situation where control of Palestine would be contested by both nationalities. Finally, the Great Powers, while protecting Christian sites, wanted neither Arab nor a Jewish state to control the Holy Basin. The Anglo-American commission in 1946 formulated that "since Palestine is a Holy Land sacred to Christian, to Jews and to Moslems alike, it should become neither an Arab state nor a Jewish state."[33] The Morrison-Grady international concept pushed for international sovereignty, stating "the area of the Holy Places should be under a trusteeship administered by the British government."[34]

Diplomats used these four factors to negotiate the internationalization of Jerusalem between 1947 and 1949. The 1936 British Peel Commission

---

31   Elie Chouraqui, *O Jerusalem*, DVD, 2006.

32   Dumper, *Politics of Jerusalem*, 18.

33   Yossi Feintuch, *U.S. Policy on Jerusalem: Contributions in Political Science* (New York: Greenwood Press, 1987), 5.

34   Ibid., 6.

recommending partition of two states in 1947 attempted to assuage all sides' fears, but the Arabs disagreed with the plan. They were fighting for all or nothing. The United Nations Partition Plan approved by the General Assembly thirty-three to thirteen on 29 November 1947 had two critical concepts, which were never implemented but have been discussed in recent peace negotiations: a two-state solution and a portion of Jerusalem as a separate international city. UNGA Resolution 181 created an Arab and an Israeli state with noncontiguous zones. While the Jewish Agency supported the two-state concept, the Arab League rejected it. Included in the approved resolution was a plan to internationalize the city of Jerusalem for ten years (see map below, UNGA Resolution 181, annex B).

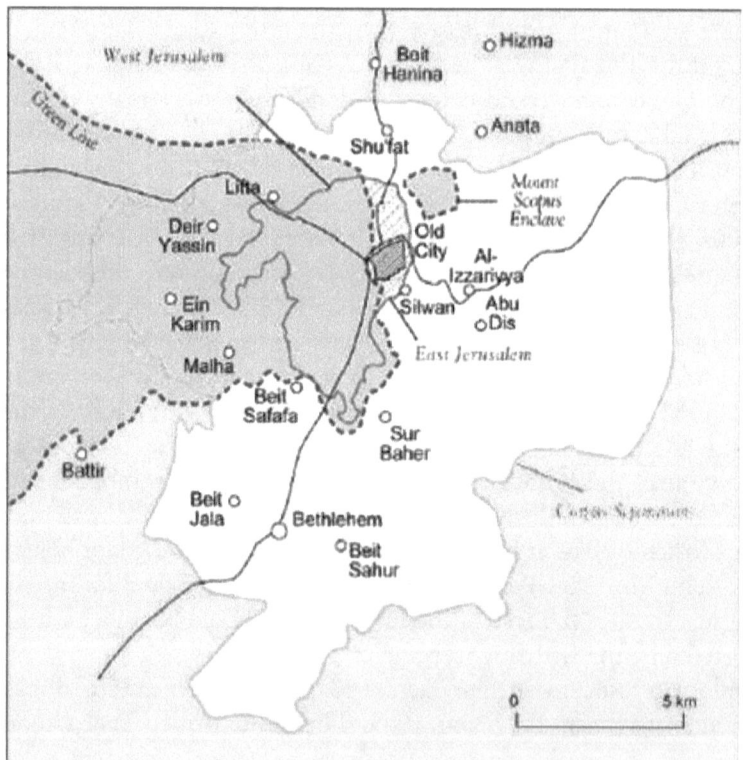

Figure 2. Corpus separatum plan for the city of Jerusalem. UNGA Resolution 181, annex B (Note: The yellow line is the greater municipality plan and the blue line is the 1949 armistice line). Source: United Nations Information System on the Question of Palestine (Washington, DC: unispal.un.org).

In UN General Agreement 181, articles 13 and 14 identified the mission of a future Jerusalem governor. Part 1, chapter 1 focused on the Holy Place concerns, which states that "the liberty of access, visit and transit shall be guaranteed, in conformity with existing rights, to all residents and citizens of the other State and of the City of Jerusalem, as well as to aliens, without distinction as to nationality, subject to requirements of national security, public order and decorum."[35] Part 3 focused on the mission of the city of Jerusalem Administering Authority for a period of ten years:

(a) To protect and to preserve the unique spiritual and religious interests located in the city of the three great monotheistic faiths throughout the world—Christian, Jewish, and Muslim—to this end to ensure that order and peace, and especially religious peace, reign in Jerusalem;

(b) To foster cooperation among all the inhabitants of the city in their own interests as well as in order to encourage and support the peaceful development of the mutual relations between the two Palestinian peoples throughout the Holy Land; to promote the security, well-being, and any constructive measures of development of the residents, having regard to the special circumstances and customs of the various peoples and communities.

Could the UN legally manage a city? The term *corpus separatum* created a controlling entity with the powers of administration and external affairs, or "an independent political entity with the authority to confer citizenship upon its residents."[36] The Vatican supported this international zone solution to protect Christian sites and maintain access while discussions occurred on the creation of Arab and Jewish states. The Vatican "was deeply gratified by the Corpus Separatum solution which could assure the growth of the city as a universal Christian Center."[37]

An international zone was a rational method to manage two competing sides who wish to control all Jerusalem. An internationally recognized governor would oversee a joint municipality with some sort of revolving local leader and council. The mandate adopted the best practices from the Ottomans while

---

[35] United Nations General Agreement 181, part 1, chapter 1, 29 November 1947, accessed 26 March 2011, http://www.un.org/documents/ga/res/2/ares2.htm.

[36] Yossi, *U.S. Policy on Jerusalem*, 14.

[37] Ibid.

preventing annexation from world powers. Resolution 181 specified a greater municipality within the proposed Arab state, with stipulations for access to the sea. The size of the international zone was predicated on including Christian sites in the Old City and Bethlehem while creating an economically viable zone. From the population data at the time, there were equal distributions of Jews and Arabs living in Jerusalem.

In May of 1948, Governor General Bernadotte and a small staff were dispatched to Jerusalem to take over the British Mandate and implement the UN Partition Plan. Obviously, he could not hold back the Palestinians who rejected the plan, nor did he have the forces to protect the Jews as they were pushed back toward the sea. The United Nations members should not have been surprised that, while withholding sovereignty from both sides, they created a violent power vacuum. "Thus, legitimacy drops out, territoriality creeps in, and external violence suddenly appears. In short, these definitional differences reflect fundamental change in the organization of violence."[38]

Unfortunately, the goal to create a viably economic city pushed the city boundary to support a greater municipality. This methodology warped the limited goal of protecting critical holy places and removed Jerusalem as the capital to any future state. The US and the UN failed to use available resources to force Jordan and Israel to remove troops from occupied Jerusalem. With the city divided for the next nineteen years, the UN continued to debate the international city utopian concept without any corresponding forcing function. Israel built up West Jerusalem as their new capital whereas Jordan focused on the increased influence from West Bankers who competed with East Bankers in Amman. The UN denied sovereignty over respective Jerusalem territories from both Israel and Jordan.

Jerusalem Sovereignty Held Hostage: UN Resolution 242

For nineteen years, the city became two distinct, separate zones, and each side took little interest in the other. In *Living Together Separately*, Michael Romann and Alex Weingrod assert that two capitals actually existed from 1948 to 1967 and were distinct and based on historical adaptation.[39] The Six-Day War from 5-11 June 1967 surprised the world and created Arab's

---

[38] Janice E. Thomson, *Mercenaries, Pirates, and Sovereigns: State-Building and Extraterritorial Violence in Early Modern Europe* (Princeton: Princeton University Press, 1994), 10.

[39] Michael Romann and Alex Weingrod, *Living Together Separately: Arabs and Jews in contemporary Jerusalem* (Princeton: Princeton University Press, 1991), 222.

second catastrophe. UN Resolution 242, issued unanimously, which has been the basis of every peace process since 1967, unfortunately does not contain previous concepts for an international zone in Jerusalem.

Michael Dumper postulates that there was a void in the international resolutions starting with UNSCR 242. The idea of an internationally backed partition was dropped to simplify the mediation after the 1967 Six-Day War. To contrast this perspective, Alan Dershowitz supports UN Resolution 242 due to the analysis of proposed changes focusing on withdrawing from "territories" instead of "the territories" or territories east of the Green Line.[40] Teddy Kollek, the Jerusalem mayor for over two decades, disagreed with the internationalization concept regarding Jerusalem. He believed that splitting a city or having a "neutral" municipality was never a long-term successful solution. Assuring access and protection was impossible due to past Arab actions and religious preferences.

What is a nation-state, and what does it control? The constitutive dimension of sovereignty "constitutes the state as the actor in the international politics by designating the state, rather than a religious or economic organization as the repository of ultimate authority with a political space that is defined territorially."[41] Israel was the first nation forced to argue stipulations during the nominative process to join the United Nations, creating a common precedent. For sixty-three years, the international community has withheld sovereignty over Israel's chosen capital and has no plans to force their course of action.

The United Nation's fight for an international city died when they did not separate the Jordanian and Israeli forces from Jerusalem in 1948, when they failed to act during the nineteen-year division, and again when Jerusalem was reunited in 1967. The larger international zone concept, if implemented today, would ignore sixty years of reality and strip sovereignty of a capital (West Jerusalem) from a state that has been a UN member since 1949. While the international community was adjusting to the new normal with Jerusalem united under Israeli sovereignty, the Arab community fought back. First was the Palestinian use of Jordan, Egypt, Syria, and Lebanon to conduct small military strikes on Israel while fighting for self-determination mainly in Jordan. Before and after the 1973 Yom Kippur or October War, Palestinians under Yasser Arafat's Palestinian Liberation Organization (PLO) were forced out of Jordan, then Lebanon, and finally arrived in Tunisia.

---

[40]   Alan Dershowitz, *The Case for Peace: How the Arab-Israeli Conflict can be Resolved* (Hoboken, New Jersey: John Wiley & Sons, 2005), 3.

[41]   Thomson, *Pirates, and Sovereigns*, 16.

To continue the peace process through future negotiations, a new capital sovereignty theory can be added to increase understanding over Jerusalem. This theory does not ignore religion or identity; it embraces all perspectives from Israelis and Palestinians while scaling down each of their interests to specific goals. Under the risk of losing access to their holy places in a Palestinian capital bounded east of the Green Line, Israel can use sovereignty over a capital and their nationally important holy places to achieve what they must have as a nation and as a people. Ben-Gurion in 1949 stated that "the State of Israel will be tested by the moral image it will lend its citizens, by the human values which will determine its internal and external relations, by its faithfulness, in deed and word, to the supreme command of Judaism: 'Thou shalt love thy neighbor as thyself.'"[42] Israeli's old one-state strategy with no external legitimacy over its capital is threatened to be replaced by a neighbor that has been granted sovereignty over two critical issues: external legitimacy over half of Jerusalem and sovereignty over holy places that define Israel's Jewish identity.

The British supported both Israelis and Arabs and ended their mandate without implementing the UN decision. Abdulateef Al-Mulhim, asking, "What if Arabs had recognized the state of Israel in 1948?" stated that "since 1948, if an Arab politician wanted to be the here and the leader of the Arab world, then he has a very easy way to do it. He just shouts as loud as he can about the intention to destroy Israel, without mobilizing one soldier—Talk is cheap . . . now the Palestinians are on their own."[43] The international community withheld sovereignty over Jerusalem from the populations affected and continues this utopian exercise today. The Six-Day War started the process to bring back the Palestinian self-determination narrative to the forefront. The next section summarizes the Arab-Israeli peace negotiations since 1973 and proposals from various institutions and think tanks.

---

[42] Avi-hai and Gurion, *State-Builder*, 45

[43] Abdulateef Al-Mulhim, "What if Arabs had recognized the State of Israel in 1948?" *Arab News*, 19 March 2011.

The Jerusalem Problem during Peace Negotiations

As all sides reacted to a new normal with Jerusalem finally united, Arab leaders and Palestinian residents fought back. This new normal brought the Palestinian narrative to the surface. The Palestinian Liberation Organization struggled to find a workable message and two intifadas by Palestinian residents forced Israelis to the negotiations table. It took eight wars and half a century for the Arabs and "the world [to] recognize we are not a negligible force."[44] The 1987 Intifada resurrected the Palestinian cause from years of failure. Arafat's support, the end of the Cold War, and the end of the Persian Gulf War led American leaders to start a peace process in Madrid in 1991. The December 1991 Madrid Conference finally brought Israelis and Palestinians to the table for the first time. The two-decade process and its impacts on Jerusalem will be addressed through an analysis of the 1993-95 Oslo negotiations and the 2000-2001 talks supported by various operational approach models seeking a final compromise.

Reaction to a One-State/One-City Environment

On 9 June 1967, Israeli forces reunited Jerusalem after nineteen years, shocking Israeli leaders and Jews throughout the world. Israel's military strength over many Arab nations created a second Arab catastrophe following the 1948 creation of the state of Israel. From 1967 to 1993, Israel attempted to integrate the Palestinian population. However, most refused full Israeli citizenship due to political considerations. Israeli leaders expanded the Jerusalem municipality to

---

44 Avi-hai and Gurion, *State-Builder*, 43.

include East Jerusalem. Annexation of East Jerusalem followed; however, Arab nations rejected Israel's offer to give back the West Bank and Gaza in exchange for peace agreements. Israel started twenty-five years attempting to integrate mixed populations while increasing Jewish growth in the municipality.

Arabs rejected the changed environment after 1967 with their policy of "Three No's" no negotiations, no recognition, and no peace.[45] The capture of all territories of the West Bank, Gaza, and East Jerusalem turned the Arab's fight for a one-Arab solution to One-Jewish solution. The failure of Nasser's 1967 war singled out the death of Pan-Arabism, and this resulted in Palestinian leaders refining their nationalistic identity. Yasser Arafat's Palestinian Liberation Organization (PLO) fought for their one-Arab state solution against Israel with incremental attacks from Egypt, Jordan, and Lebanon's territory. Palestinian refugees had drastically changed Jordanian demographics, and the PLO's emergence created a power struggle against the Jordanian king as well as with Israel. Surrounding nations attempted to support the PLO but not anger a now-powerful Israel. Syria supported the PLO's overthrow of Jordan but did not support PLO attacks on Israel from their soil. Jordan succeeded in defeating PLO extremist groups and kicked out the PLO to Lebanon. The PLO created havoc in Lebanon, and a violent civil war led to Israel's 1982 invasion, defeat, and expulsion of the PLO. Arab governments were isolating Israel diplomatically. Anwar Sadat of Egypt succeeded to change the Arab negotiating balance through the 1973 October War and became the first Arab leader to sign a peace treaty with Israel.

Both sides reacted to support their own interests. In 1980, Israel formally annexed East Jerusalem while, in 1988, Yasser Arafat declared Palestinian independence. Rashid Khalidi, an advisor to the Palestinian delegation during the 1991 Madrid negotiations, described the Palestinian narrative's disappearance and reemergence. The disappearance of Palestinian nationalism has four contextual reasons. The first is when half of the Arab population fled to Palestine after the first Arab-Israeli war in 1948, or what Arabs call al-Nakba or the catastrophe. The second is the Palestinian integration into surrounding Arab societies, stirring up internal conflict when they would not integrate and when full citizenship was denied for political reasons. This continued as revolts in Jordan and Lebanon as the leadership was forced to flee to Tunisia in 1982. Thirdly, Pan-Arabism kept the nationalistic movement broad until crushed in 1967. The Cold War was the fourth factor, which separated friendly

---

[45] "The Three No's of Khartoum," accessed 25 March 2011, http://www.sixdaywar. org/content/khartoum.asp.

Western-leaning Arab countries from Arab countries who leaned toward the Soviet Union. Rashid Khalidi called the organized a collection of "Arabs as a single people," and "Arab nationalism . . . had become a powerful symbolic bogeyman, representing all that was objectionable in the Arab world to those outside it."[46]

Israel had two strategic choices to balance regarding East Jerusalem: separation or integration. To explain the importance of Jerusalem demographics, "it is no surprise that Israeli's conscious policy since 1967 has been to 'limit the growth of the Arab population of the city.'"[47]Israel chose policies that ensured a seventy-thirty demographic split in Jerusalem. Israeli officials followed "a strict quota on construction for Arabs in the city that has been enforced for more than twenty years with the aim of maintaining the Palestinian percentage of the city's residents at around 26 percent."[48] As an Arab advisor for Jerusalem mayor Teddy Kollek, Amir Cheshin described the lack of development for East Jerusalem. Surprisingly, this evidence is similar to the lack of development in Jordan-controlled East Jerusalem from 1948 to 1967. To limit the higher natural growth rate of Palestinians, administrators focused on land zoning "by setting a strict limit on new homes built in [Arab] neighborhoods."[49]

As a scholar for the Institute for Palestine Studies, Geoffrey Aronson asserts that Labor Party leader Yitzhak Rabin was only following the same Likud settlement policies pushed for the last ten years, using security and "territorial continuity" that linked isolated Jewish settlements especially on the outer ring to the inner ring of West Jerusalem. Arial Sharon and Ehud Olmert followed the same policy, supporting the construction of two new towns called Har Homa and Gilo in 1997. Palestinian think tanks, such as the Palestinian Academic Society for the Study of International Affairs, track the daily housing changes to include the growth of settlements, *dumahs* exchanged, and respective populations in Jerusalem districts. The twelve Israeli settlements built in East Jerusalem, which are governed by the Jerusalem municipality with West Jerusalem, include Gilo, Har Homa, Har Gilo, Mamilla, East Talpiot,

---

[46] Rashid Khalidi, *Palestinian Identity: The Construction of Modern National Consciousness* (New York: Columbia University Press, 1997), 184.

[47] Marshall J. Breger and Ora Ahimeir. *Jerusalem: A City and Its Future* (New York: Syracuse University Press, 2002), 5.

[48] Geoffrey Aronson, *Final Status Issues* (Jerusalem: Institute for Palestine Studies, 1996), 18.

[49] Amir Cheshin, Bill Hutman, and Avi Melamed, *Separate and Unequal* (Jerusalem: Harvard University Press, 1999), 30.

Giv'at Shappira, Mount Scopus, Neve Ya'akov, Pisgat Ze'ev, Ramat Eshkol, Ma'ale Zeitim, and Pisgat Amir.[50]

If the one-state concept failed to reflect both perspectives, then correspondingly the one-city concept failed to reflect two distinct cities, a Jewish Jerusalem and a Palestinian Jerusalem. The lack of peace-talk progress, continued settlements in East Jerusalem, and the rise of Hamas has "rejuvenated the old idea of one bi-national, secular and democratic state where Jewish and Arab citizens live side by side in equality . . . many Palestinian think a single state might be ideal—since it would involve the defeat of the Zionist project and its replacement by a bi-national country that would eventually be ruled by its Arab majority."[51] This argument is based on demographic evidence as a method to distort Israeli's claim to their one-state system since 1967. However, Arabs such as the Palestinian Strategy Group use it to "warn Israel of the dangers posed by its expansionist polices . . . believes that one-state talk might help knock some sense into the heads of Israeli decision-makers."[52]

The proposal to convert all Palestine back to Arab control delegitimizes Israeli interests and reverses sixty-three years of nationhood. This may seem extreme, but it reflects Palestinian frustrations over Israel's one-city control and one-state control. This argument is based on whether a democratic state follows representative government, highlighting the importance of demographics. Countless groups, including Israeli-based Peace Now and B'Tselem, use demographic growth numbers to explain why Israel, under their one-state concept, cannot maintain majority representation over both Israelis and Palestinians into the future. Writing for the Institute for Palestinian Studies, Michael Dumper spends countless pages explaining two conclusions: that Palestinian natural birth increase will continue to outpace Israeli natural birth rates, and that decreasing Jewish immigration was the only method that kept the current population ratios where they are today.

Both Israelis and Palestinians delegitimize each other to argue their case. There are elements of denial from both extremes. Chairman Arafat's comments at the 2000 Camp David Summit, "That the Jewish Temple had never been located on the Al-Haram al-Sharif," caused a failure of those July 2000 negotiations.[53] References to the Battle of Khaybar when Jews were expelled

---

[50] *Jerusalem: Israeli Settlement Activities and Related Polices* (Jerusalem: Palestinian Academic Society for the Study of International Affairs, June 2009).

[51] "The One State Solution," *Newsweek*, 20 September 2008.

[52] Ibid.

[53] Marshall Breger, *Jerusalem: A City and its Future* (Syracuse: Jerusalem Institute for Israel Studies, 2002), 7.

from Arabia in the seventh century are used by extremists to show that Islam will never accept a Jewish state.[54]

Israelis use the same tactics when they question whether there is any such term as *Palestinian narrative*. The Israeli political group One Jerusalem does not want their historic Jerusalem divided. They assume away Palestinian's self-determination and ignore Arab East Jerusalem's low level of development. Peace negotiations will always fail when each side ignores the other's interests. "The one-state solution is advocated by a number of Palestinian intellectuals and is becoming rather popular in the European left."[55] The American Task Force for Palestine has even published a book describing the counterintuitive effects this negotiating tactic has on the peace process, titled *What's Wrong with the One-State Solution*.[56] This one-state dialogue is used for three reasons: as a negotiations tactic to create fear for Israelis, to force them to the negotiations table, and as dialogue to express Palestinian frustration.

An Incremental Process Led to the 1993-95 Oslo Peace Talks

The context leading to the 1993 talks include incremental peace talks with Egypt, end of the Cold War, the 1991 Persian Gulf, and the return of Palestinian self-determination. The 1978 Camp David Accords and the 1993 Oslo talks may have failed to address Jerusalem and all Palestinian problems; however, they focused instead on achieving limited, incremental agreements. During the Dayton Peace negotiations that ended the Bosnian War, Richard Holbrooke "rejected the minimalist theory that we should negotiate only those matters on which implementation would be relatively easy."[57] However, the Bosnian negotiations and Sarajevo are simple when compared to a contested city for the world's three monotheistic religions. Peace talks that consider Jerusalem as too complicated does stretch the conflict; however, incremental peace agreements have created a new peace environment and have improved negotiations that reflect the interests of each side.

During the Oslo I (1993) and Oslo II or Taba discussions (1995), the international community recognized the PLO as the Palestinian legitimate representative and granted the new Palestinian Authority limited sovereignty

---

54 Steven Simpson, "Islam will never accept Jewish State," *American Thinker*, 30 Jun 2010.

55 "The Challenges of a One-State Solution," *Haaretz*, 20 June 2010.

56 Hussein Ibish, *What's Wrong with the One-State Solution* (Washington, DC: American Task Force on Palestine, 2009), 1.

57 Richard Holbrook, *To End a War* (New York: The Modern Library, 1999), 205.

over three areas in the West Bank, Gaza, and East Jerusalem. Negotiations focused on the status of Jewish towns built in East Jerusalem, reaffirmed by Oslo II, that they "would under no circumstances be placed under Palestinian authority, even in criminal matters."[58]

The 1968 PLO Charter demands an Arab-led one-state solution. Israel has perpetuated their one-state concept by ignoring the rise of Palestinian self-determination. Palestinians highlight that a separate independent Palestinian state next to a state of Israel will be weak. By incorporating Jewish population centers, weak resources will be dominated by a strong Israeli neighbor, and issues like right of return may be distinguished. Abu Mazen has suggested that all historical requirements would be taken off the table once they had a state of Palestine (reference). ATFP and Hussein Ibish hint that the one-state agenda as a negotiating tactic visualizes a future to Israelis on the risk of no final two-state agreement. [59]

The Tel Aviv University's Jaffee Center for Strategic Studies (JCSS) published six models in 1989, but few focused on the effects or on the importance of Jerusalem. The models were summarized as the Status Quo, Autonomy, Annexation, a Palestinian State, Gaza Withdrawal, and a Jordanian-Palestinian Federation. The 1993 accords followed the autonomy model by creating both the PNA and the three authority zones, while Jordan handed over all sovereign claims over the West Bank to the PNA. The underlying framework end states were to "allow Israel to end its control over more than 1.5 million Palestinians."[60] The models left only the creation of a Palestinian state, which "offers a greater possibility of resolving the Palestinian issue on terms acceptable to the Palestinians than does any other option considered."[61] However, trading land for peace with the rejection of any Jews living in an Arab zone as illegal, "six wars in 40 years, and 70 years of Arab terrorism have left their mark on the collective subconscious of Israeli society."[62]

A follow-on JCSS study in 1995 by Dr. Dore Gold summarized three new models for Jerusalem: Territorial, Religious, and Municipal. The territorial

---

[58] Aronson, *Final Status Issues*, 31. The Palestinian Authority was granted control over area A, or approximately 20 percent of the contested areas, Gaza and Jericho. Area B included Palestinian control but Israeli military access. Area C was under Israeli control.

[59] Ibish, *One-State Solution*, 1.

[60] Jaffee Center for Strategic Studies Study Group. *The West Bank and Gaza: Israel's Options for Peace*. (Tel Aviv: JCSS, 1989), 18.

[61] Ibid., 15.

[62] Ibid., 185.

model creates two sovereign capitals with vast differences over which side controls the Temple Mount, the Western Wall, and the rest of the Old City. Any respective leader that does not retain sovereignty over the Temple Mount and the Western Wall would lose internal legitimacy of its people. There was no discussion of a Holy Basin zone, but three reasons were listed to create such a zone for the Old City. The first is the potential limited religious freedom "out of consideration that the area of the Wall itself was part of an old Islamic Waqf."[63] Secondly, when Jordan controlled the Old City from 1948 to 1967, all Jews were evicted and Jewish holy sites were desecrated, which resulted in no international condemnation. Thirdly, Palestinian sovereignty over the Haram al-Sharif defines their identity, far more than the small Arab towns in East Jerusalem.

Under the municipal or religious models, with Israel's full control over greater Jerusalem, Muslims would retain local management of any waqf holy place. The municipal model provides local autonomy to the Palestinian boroughs as they do now. The report summarized the difficulty Jerusalem causes regarding the other final status issues, which asked, "Might not the Jerusalem issue wreck the rest of peace process?[64] Dr. Gold had difficulty even as recent as 1995 to focus on Jerusalem, and he continuously rejected an option to divide Jerusalem in order to create distinct capitals with secured borders. Many of these joint, bilateral governmental solutions sound very rational but ignore the historical background, importance of international involvement, or the realistic ability to solve day-to-day problems if larger political issues are unresolved. Much of the detailed planning to turn Arab East Jerusalem into a capital for the future state of Palestine has been accomplished, but the larger political and sovereign issues have not been addressed.

The end of the Cold War changed statecraft, and experts highlighted the end of war, conquest, and annexation. Francis Fukuyama postulated that statecraft changed in the 1990s with humanitarian assistance used as an excuse to change or adapt internal state systems, degrading state sovereignty.[65] Kosovo and East Timor were new states created by combinations of armed conflict and diplomacy, following Charles Hill's assertion that "diplomacy precedes the state"[66] The first intifada created an international crisis that attempted

---

63   Ibid., 26.
64   Dore Gold, *Jerusalem Final Status* (Tel Aviv: Jaffee Center for Strategic Studies, 1995), 45.
65   Francis Fukuyama, *State-Building* (Ithaca, New York: Cornell University Press, 2004), 39.
66   Hill, *Grand Strategies*, 10.

to change Israel's internal status quo. The return of Palestinian nationalism through revolt, the failure of improvements for East Jerusalem citizens, and international diplomacy granting some sovereignty to a new Palestinian entity started the path to statehood.

Scaling into the Two-State Concept: 2000-2001 Discussions

The context leading to the 2000 talks include the 1993 achievements, the 1995 Oslo II timelines, and the assassination of Rabin, which changed internal Israeli politics forever. As a scholar for the Jerusalem Institute for Israeli Studies, Menachem Klein summarized the 2000-2001 Camp David discussions using comparable negotiation models from Northern Ireland and South African peace talks. John Darby and Roger MacGinty list five criteria for a successful negotiation: negotiations in good faith, the inclusion of all key actors to include paramilitary groups, central issues must be addressed, no use of force to achieve objectives, and a commitment to a sustained process. All but the third issue "were missing or deformed in the [2000] Israeli-Palestinian permanent status talks."[67]

In 2009, the Palestinian Authority published a two-year government plan to prepare the government, the Palestinians, and the international community, showing the world that statehood is a possibility. The plan addresses resource shortfalls and approaches to create sustainability within education, economic markets, justice, and public utilities. Due to these preparations, Palestinian expectations were rising before the self-imposed two-year plan culminates. M. G. Moeller, an air force general leading the United States Security Coordinator Office (USSC), is charged with helping support the creation and training of ten Palestinian security battalions. More recently, Israel political changes to a Likud-led government may in fact bring on board the far right political parties. Many suggested that Labor is more giving to "land for peace," but they may not have had the population support. In contrast, the Palestinian Authority are prepared to offer hope to Israelis, but they were as fractured.

The Palestinian National Authority asserts that East Jerusalem must be their future capital as it is contiguous with their West Bank populations. Oslo negotiations highlighted that once political solutions are chosen, city municipalities, PLO governments, and even the future state would require more capacity, resources, and professionalism. Once the United States supported a two-state solution, they had to back up ideas with resources. Michael Dumper's thesis in *The Politics of Jerusalem Since 1967* is "that a durable peace and the

---

[67] Menachem Klein, *The Jerusalem Problem* (Gainesville: University Press of Florida), 3.

security and prosperity of both peoples—Israeli and Palestinian—depend not only on the creation of a viable Palestinian state but also on a formula assuring a shared Jerusalem in which both can have their capital."[68]

European countries and the United States began a multilevel effort to tackle complexity and true nation building through institution building separate from the Middle East peace initiatives. The Aspen Institute, Overseas Private Investment Corporation, and the Palestinian Investment Fund were incorporated into a Middle East investment initiative to synchronize and prioritize World Bank and donor resources and effort, including a $228 million loan guarantee in 2007.[69] To support the message that the United States is a neutral actor after years of providing billions to Israeli support, the United States now provides close to $600 million to the PNA yearly.[70] President George W. Bush and Secretary of State Condoleezza Rice in 2007 created the US-Palestinian Partnership (UPP) to improve economic incentives and development within Gaza and the West Bank. Complementing the PNA reform agendas, UPP's initiatives are focused on three sectors: information and communication technology, hotel and tourism, and agribusiness. Prime Minister Salam Fayyad, who created the Palestinian Reform and Development Plan (PRDP), greatly supported the projects "that have a sustainable development effect on the economy. We are supporting the Palestinian private sector and their international counterparts to mobilize investments to create jobs."[71]

This focus on economic capacity building is one line of effort advocating the end of the Middle East conflict. The 2003 nonpartisan, not-for-profit American Task Force for Palestine "has developed lines of communications with the US, Palestinian, Israeli and Jordanian governments in order to pursue its policy advocacy goals."[72] Supporting the official policy of the United States, Secretary of State Hillary Clinton asserted that "a two-state solution would mean an independent, viable, and sovereign state of their own and your own;

---

[68] Dumper, *Politics of Jerusalem*, 3.

[69] US-Palestinian Partnership, accessed on January 2011, http://www.uspalestinianpartnership.org.

[70] State Department Diplomatic Note, "Secretary Clinton announces budge assistance for the Palestinian Authority." November 10, 2010, accessed 17 March 2010, http://www.state.gov/.

[71] Salam Fayyad to Mr. Isaccson, Letter from the Prime Minister's Office (Ramallah: The Aspen Institute, 24 November 2007).

[72] American Task Force on Palestine (ATFP), accessed on 01 September 2010, http://www.american task force on Palestine.

the freedom to travel, to do business, and govern themselves. Palestinians would have the right to chart their own destinies at last."[73] In a letter to the ATFP president, Dr. Ziad Asali, during the fifth annual gala, president of the state of Palestine Mahmoud Abbas stated "the theme of your gathering—'Building Palestine, the Indispensible State for Peace'—has become an imperative that enjoys the widest international acceptance and support . . . the United States contributes economically and financially in supporting the institutions of the Palestinian National Authority."[74]

To manage the $7.7 billion pledged from the 2007 Paris Donors Conference, the Palestinian Authority prepared a Palestinian Reform and Development Plan (PRDP), supported by the United States and European Union, with four key sectors: governance, social affairs, economic and private sector development, and infrastructure. The Europe press release broke down these sectors:[75]

Economic and private sector development: trade facilitation, small and medium enterprises guarantee and financing, business centers, quick-impact projects such as those proposed by the Quartet Special Representative Tony Blair as well as payment of private sector areas.

Two Capitals Require a Divided Jerusalem: A Win-Win

From the three utopian concepts previously listed, diplomats have frowned upon a divided city and especially a divided capital. Before 1948, it can be argued that Jerusalem was a mixed ethnic city, but the environment changed over time due to war, external influence, and armistice. The history of dividing and then reuniting Berlin showed that however practical a division may seem during conflict, division is both temporary and harmful. To think contrarian, negotiators can adopt "temporary" divisions to change the status quo, perspectives, and biases.

To understand long term consequences and mitigation measures for two separate cities side by side, historical processes must be examined. Examples of

---

[73] Hillary Clinton, "Speech at the American Task Force for Palestine Fifth Annual Gala," Washington, DC, 20 October 2010.

[74] Mahmud Abbas to Dr. Ziad Asali, Letters from the Palestinian President (Ramallah: American Task Force on Palestine, 13 October 2010. (The author attended the fifth annual dinner on 20 October 2010).

[75] PEGASE and the PRDP, Europe press release, Memo 48/08 (Brussels: Europa, 28 January 2008), accessed on 17 March 2011, http://europa.eu/rapid/pressReleasesAction.

divided cities include Beirut, Belfast, Lahore, Trieste, and Punjab.[76] A defined and secured border between West and East Jerusalem contributes to increased security; however, academics focus on long-term consequences. Jon Calame, Esther Charlsworth, and Lebbeus Woods state that urban divisions are not cost-effective in the long-term. By using Iraq's safe neighborhood barriers that stopped tribal killings, Calame's municipal solutions and evidence of long-term border liabilities include "duplication of facilities and services—as seen in Nicosia, Jerusalem, and Mostar in particular—puts unnatural pressure on municipal budgets."[77] Secured borders create positive benefits, to include displacing violence, but never achieve the complete end of violence. Of course, violence is a symptom of underlying problems, but no alternative solutions are provided when different ethnic groups kill one another. They are correct that temporary or transitional measures, like the Berlin wall, easily become permanent, but changes in people and societies are generational changes.

The fight for keeping Jerusalem united is a scaled version of the one-state solution. Using history to cite a stretched narrative, Jewish leaders assert, "Jerusalem has existed for 3,000 years as Israel's capital . . . Never again, they say, can the city be divided and Jews be forbidden to pray before their holiest shrine, the Wailing Wall."[78] Regarding settlements, Palestinian negotiators recognize that they do not want to control Jewish towns in East Jerusalem. As far as cost of destruction or removal, Jews living in apartment buildings or "small tower and stable" settlements are negligible. Moving thousand-person cities such as those in and around the Jerusalem municipality are incalculable. Can the UN pay for the relocation of two hundred thousand Israelis out of East Jerusalem to make the city ethnically pure while not paying for the relocation of Palestinians? The peace process, with the two-state solution as the central theme, "ends a lengthy period of mutual denial, when both sides withheld recognition as if it were the ultimate weapon."[79]

Israel had its chance for their one-state solution. Early infrastructure investment for Arab towns within East Jerusalem was reported to be as low as 4 percent.[80] Current investment numbers, reported by the East Jerusalem

---

[76]   Ian Talbot, *Divided Cities: Partition and its aftermath in Lahore and Amritsar, 1947-1957* (London: Oxford University Press, 2004), 1.

[77]   Jon Calame, Esther Charlesworth, and Lebbeus Woods, *Divided Cities: Belfast, Beirut, Jerusalem, Mostar and Nicosia* (Philadelphia: University of Pennsylvania Press, 13 March 2009), 241.

[78]   "Israel: Unifying a Divided City," *Time Magazine*, 20 November 1978.

[79]   Khalidi, 204.

[80]   Cheshin, 34.

administrator, are up to 20-35 percent and can be explained through three legitimate factors. The first is that the population refuses to recognize or cooperate with Israeli leaders, second is the internal backlash, and the third is the fear that Israeli improvement, however legitimate, will cause permanent political changes to the environment.[81]

Israel has been in danger by creating a democratic state based on an assumed demographic seventy-thirty split. Israel supports the concept that "West Jerusalem and twelve Jewish neighborhoods that are home to 200,000 residents will be ours. The Arab neighborhoods in which close to a quarter million Palestinians live will be theirs," as described by Ehud Barak on 2 September 2010.[82] Palestinians despise the concept since the settlement process may never stop and may even split the West Bank. After 1967, Israel had a chance to build a united city but could never rely on demographics to remain largely Jewish. Policies were "directed towards increasing the numbers of Israeli Jews and restricting those of Palestinian Arabs in the new borders of united Jerusalem."[83]

To understand why a united Jerusalem increased the conflict, Dr. Gold suggested three factors. First, UN Resolution 242, issued on November 1967, did not discuss Palestine or Jerusalem as a nation's capital. Dr. Gold also points out that the European Union's increased their activity to improve East Jerusalem "which has its own political agenda connected to the re-division of Jerusalem, then this amounts to interference in the internal affairs of Israel, especially when this effort so completely contradicts the policy of Israel's democratically elected government."[84] The European Union supported East Jerusalem recognition without ever offering recognition of West Jerusalem as Israel's capital, or mutual recognition. Thirdly, the increase in Sunni extremists has highlighted that the international community's contradicting actions are turning over control of Jerusalem holy places over to one group, currently a nonstate entity. The European Union's favoritism for the Palestinian narrative has led to bigotry against Israel, which has complicated negotiations. The extremist takeover of Gaza after Israel removed every settlement showed the world what emerging threats remain to holy place access and protection for all religions.

---

81 Interview with Mr. Yakir Segev, Israeli East Jerusalem administrator, Jerusalem, 17 January 2011.

82 Ari Shavit, "Barak to Haaratz: Israel Ready to Cede Parts of Jerusalem in Peace Deal," *Haaretz*, 2 September 2010.

83 Dumper, *Politics of Jerusalem*, 11.

84 Dore Gold, *The Fight for Jerusalem* (Washington, DC: Dore Gold Books, 2007), 259.

While the Palestinian Authority is hopeful that negotiations will bring a state of Palestine, Israelis have difficulty looking beyond the continuous fear they have lived with since 1948. There are two narratives in people, their fears and their hopeful opportunities, "but when this longed-for opportunity finally is being realized, fear often comes to constitute a major psychological obstacle to the achievement of peace."[85] Israel must be offered a future that includes international legitimacy, peace, and sovereignty over those holy places that define them as a people. A working methodology must include the Israeli and Palestinian transformation from fear to hope. The Palestinian chief negotiator Saeb Erakat has informed the United Nations that the Palestinian Authority will ask the United Nations to recognize a Palestinian state within the 1967 borders, with full membership—and with East Jerusalem as its capital—in order to "seek an alternative as negotiations with Israel were not going anywhere."[86]

---

[85] Daniel Bar-Tal, "Why Does Fear Override Hope in Societies Engulfed by Intractable Conflict, as it does in the Israeli Society," *Political Psychology* 22-3 (2010), 602.

[86] Saeb Erakat, "Erekat: We will Seek UN Recognition Soon," *Ma'an News Agency.* 21 March 2011.

An International
Holy Basin Methodology
to Bridge Differences

In the *Sum of All Fears*, Tom Clancy's 1991 novel described a fictional joint administration for Jerusalem, managed by an Imam, a rabbi, and a cardinal.[87] Security was provided by Swiss Guards, the same guards that secure the Vatican and have historical ties to one of the first professional forces after the Dark Ages. This joint methodology can be legitimized by the international community seeking an end to the Arab-Israeli-Palestinian conflict. This fictional setting used a combination of strategies that are sometimes unspeakable but cause readers to ask why not. Some of the latest proposals have barely touched on subjects such as security force loyalties, their legitimacy, and the difficult mission to provide access to all religions.

The strategy of sovereignty contradicts ideas and strategies for an open, free, and demilitarized Jerusalem. Open and free city terminology has been used during past conflicts, either resulting from war or confrontation between nations. "In the last century, cities such as Shanghai, Danzig, and Trieste were free cities . . . Perhaps a similar philosophy can apply to the troubled region in the Middle East."[88] The following paragraphs will identify positive aspects that an international Holy Basin provides to holy areas that may forever remain in contention.

---

[87] Tom Clancy, *The Sum of All Fears* (New York: Berkley Books, 1991), 1.

[88] Patrick Truax, "A New Tack in the Holy Land." *Digital Journal*, 29 December 2008, accessed on 15 March 2011, http://www.digitaljournal.com/article/264175#ixzz1GDLdInrt.

No one wants to divide a city. From historical experience, every time that has occurred has only been a temporary and unforgiving solution. Berlin comes to mind with its forty-nine-year split that defined the Cold War. However, there are three reasons to contemplate a divided Jerusalem that creates two distinct and secure capitals. These are to protect rights of many stakeholders, provide a rational method for a joint Holy Basin or Old City municipality, and break the peace negotiation impasse. The European Union government focuses strategy and resources on East Jerusalem as a future PA capital that leads to dividing Jerusalem as two capitals. Public discourse must incorporate a two-capital concept to support the two-state concept, with detailed discussion on which holy places have overlapping interests to two or more religious groups. An analysis of two models will set parameters around the Jerusalem problem. The University of Windsor Old City Initiative focuses on the critical issue of the Old City with a joint proposal that approaches an exact version of sovereignty. The Holy Basin model proposed by the Jerusalem Institute for Israeli Studies in 2010 includes the other three overlapping holy places near the Old City but leaves out important emerging strategies that would result.

Where to Place the Boundaries: The Old City Initiative

There is a way to geographically link the Jewish quarter, parts of the Armenian quarter, and the Western Wall to West Jerusalem, but as was stated before, the Temple Mount is holy, not the Western Wall. To scale down from an impossible extreme of cutting up the Temple Mount into sovereign sections, think tanks and universities have sought out a methodology to improve negotiations. Extreme sovereignty may never be possible. Until each side agrees to cut up the Old City, this creates a new temporary normal.

The University of Windsor has created the Jerusalem Old City Initiative, or JOCI, with detailed planning on what a "special regime" would incorporate.[89] Identifying the many interests, stakeholders, and historical reasons, the Old City and other holy places cannot be split or only given to one side. This joint regime recognizes reality on the ground. "The optimal solution is an Old City 'special regime,' founded on agreed norms of international law, established at the direction of both Palestine and Israel."[90] This joint municipality model is temporary and leaves the issue of sovereignty open. In effect, the concept

---

[89] Mazen Qupty, *The Legal Framework for a Special Regime: The Old City of Jerusalem* (Ontario, Canada: University of Windsor, 2010), 1.

[90] Michael J. Molloy, Michael Bell, and Join Bell, *Governance Discussion Document* (Ontario, Canada: University of Windsor, 2008), 3.

removes religious interests and sovereignty issues from negotiations but would be negated if any UN resolution defines an Arab East Jerusalem as sovereign to a Palestinian state. A chief administrator would be charged with the critical missions of access, protection, and security.

A joint administration with some form of rotating elections and strong security forces would manage the competing demands of equity with security. Key tasks include governance, access, law and order, archeology, land management, and services; but many shared tasks would include citizenship, legal, infrastructure, and utilities. This is the soft border concept that Yossi Feintuch describes while understanding a nation's requirements to protect their sovereign borders and people. The security force provided by a third party, due to the lack of trust, would still have to coordinate with the respective national security services of each state. From an interview with the Israeli East Jerusalem mayor, he doubted the availability, training, and willingness of a foreign security officer or soldier to physically protect an Israeli citizen from a suicide bomber.[91]

Palestinian-American community leader Ray Hanania, while announcing his candidacy for the Palestinian Authority in 2009, asserted that "Jerusalem should be a shared city and Palestinians should have an official presence in East Jerusalem. The Old City should be shared by both permitting open access to the city to all with a joint Palestinian-Israeli police presence."[92] While demanding sovereignty over East Jerusalem, Mr. Hanania ignores the requirements for a state government to control its borders and assumes a joint Israeli-Palestinian government would be feasible.

What does an outside boundary do? It denies free access from the state to its capital. It denies sovereignty to a nation's declared capital. Internal legitimacy from a population demands that a state controls key sites important to its national and religious identity. Israel currently has sovereignty and internal legitimacy over all Jerusalem, but the international community has

---

[91]   Interview with Yakir Segev, East Jerusalem Municipality administrator, Jerusalem, 20 January 2011.

[92]   Ray Hanania, "A Peace Plan for All of Us," *Mideast Web*, 2 December 2009.

denied external legitimacy over Jerusalem as a capital to Israel. Jordan was also denied international legitimacy over East Jerusalem, and for the time being, the UN has also denied a capital to the PNA. However, the push to create a state of Palestine with sovereignty over all East Jerusalem based on the Green Line alone would strip sovereignty from a standing UN country.

Protecting the rights of multiple stakeholders had defined Jerusalem's negotiating history: With three religions, only an ugly gerrymandered solution is possible to cut up each holy place to their respective religious base, but what to do when multiple religions consider the same site sacred? The early push for internationalization was caused by the European powers attempting to protect mainly Christian sides as the two populations demanded a level of nationalism. They wanted to keep Jewish or Arab dominating control of the holy places out of the hands of a single group that could oppress or restrict the other side. The mandate and the international city concept was a temporary solution only; UN General Agreement (UNGA) Resolution 181 used a ten year interval period with a subsequent review process.

A Holy Basin Zone Reflects Reality and Multiple Stakeholders

There are two overall models of where to place the boundaries—on the outside municipal boundary or on the inside that protects key holy places. A greater Jerusalem would have some level of boundaries on the outside, preventing free access from two states into their designated capitals. This denies sovereignty over a nation's capital. This international concept includes utopian ideas such as an *undivided, open and demilitarized*. The only way to maintain both would be to have boundaries to control, at the minimum passport control and access. Which laws would the citizens be under, Sharia or Jewish law? Who would have arrest authority, and who could prosecute?

Issue of Sovereignty: denies sovereignty over a nation's own capital. The United States did not want to use troops to create an international city during the 1948 partition debates. Now, the United States wants to strip sovereignty from Israel and hand it over to another "quasi-state entity," breaking over sixty years of US policy, preventing only one nation from controlling most of the holy places.

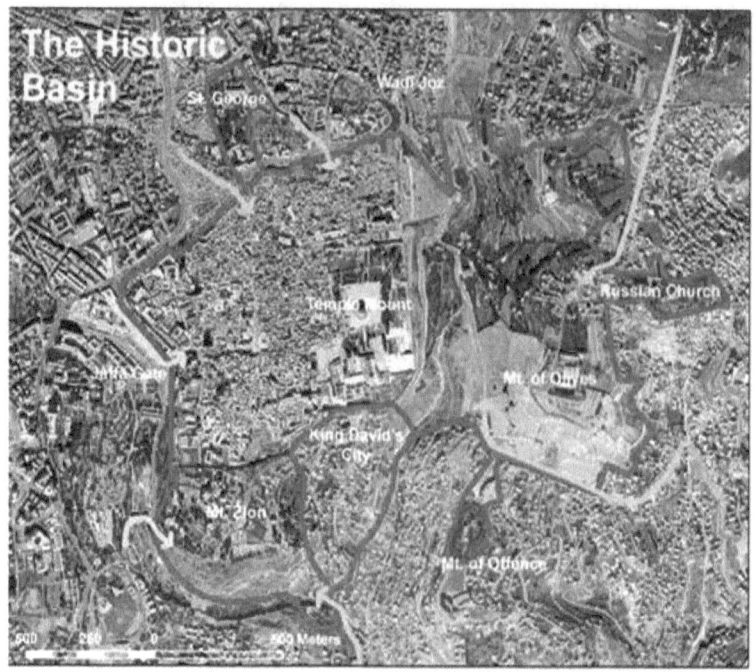

Figure 3. Proposed Holy Basin boundary. Reproduced
with permission from Ruth Lapidoth, *The Historic Basin of
Jerusalem—Problems and Possible Solutions* (Jerusalem: Jerusalem
Institute for Israeli Studies, 2010), 9.

Bilateral Negotiations Do Not Provide International Legitimacy

The idea of a bilateral agreement seems rational by removing any appearance of US influence and by not forcing a resolution that may not be agreeable to the respective populations. However, the first factor underlies the need to work with regional and international agencies even if the United States does not take the lead role. Negotiations must be international, not bilateral, due to multiple reasons. The Palestinians have nothing to offer Israel. It is the international community, influenced by the twenty-two Arab League countries, that maintains the sovereignty cards over Jerusalem and recognition of Israel as a sovereign nation state.[93] Israel cannot grant international sovereignty to Palestinians and have no reason to hand over the sovereignty over half of

---

[93] Arab League Members, accessed on 17 March 2011, http://www.arab.de/arabinfo/league/.

Jerusalem when West Jerusalem sovereignty is denied to Israel. The fact is that bilateral talks are useless, and the world community must be involved since they hold the cards that Israelis and Palestinians desire.

The United Nations community created the problem when they did not enforce the partition plan after Britain ended her mandate and when they withheld sovereignty over Jerusalem from both Israel and Jordan. International recognition is required to end the history of over sixty UN resolutions that withhold Jerusalem sovereignty from Israeli governments. The United Nations Trust Supervision Organization, even with its inadequacies, is the administration that has overseen ceasefires from Israel, Lebanon, Jordan, Syria, and Egypt since 1949, has expertise, has contacts, and understands the terrain. Their 2010 yearly budget was over $60 million, and one would think that amount of money could be better spent to support a peace proposal and not perpetuate sixty-three years of confrontation.[94]

Israel's perceived UN biases may be overblown; however, this historical perception cannot be ignored with dozens of resolutions over dozens of years critical to Israel. The Quartet, as an overarching third party, does help the negotiation process by providing more legitimacy than the United Nations alone. The United States has a critical role that has helped incremental agreements, which has produced far more peaceful nation-state intercourse. The European Union, through a 2006 document, has recognized the need to be an honest broker. "The American strategy to advance, or now restore, the Peace Process, essentially takes advantage of the superpower status of the United States, who can impose themselves as the only external indispensable player in the Israeli-Palestinian game."[95] Many of the latest studies start with a fundamental factor and incorporate realities on the ground. JOCI focuses only on the Old City and incorporates the soft border concept. This protects only those sites that have overlap. A Holy Basin expanded to include the Mount of Olives, Mount Scopus, and UNTSO areas that include the consulate district north of the Old City called Sheik Jarrah.

Israel cannot argue the one-state solution and ignore 30 percent of their population. Israeli leaders must go beyond the twenty-five-meter close fight and seek out a future strategy that secures external legitimacy over a defined capital, a state not threatened by demographics and sovereignty over key holy

---

94 United Nations Trust Supervision Organization, accessed 21 March 2011, http://wwwupdate.un.org/en/peacekeeping/missions/untso/facts.

95 Dorothee Schmid, "Mapping European and American Economic Initiatives towards Israel and the Palestinian Authority and their Effects on Honest Broker Perceptions," *EuroMESCO 61* (October 2006), 8.

places. A third zone with international guarantees for protection and access is a methodology to incorporate both Palestinian and Israeli perspectives and interests.

There is a potential for compromise if each side recognizes and protects their respective interests. A temporary proposal can build a new normal while protecting the interests of both. The less powerful side must provide trust. Klein provides examples from Northern Ireland and South African negotiations. Until delegitimization ends, Israelis will not be able to trust their holiest sites within a future East Jerusalem Palestinian capital. A separate Holy Basin zone temporarily removes the trust factor, placing sovereignty into an internationally-recognized entity. This incremental approach must not be rejected or scorned but embraced in order to create new understanding. The benefits of international recognition, with Palestinian self-determination finally realized, will obviously create emerging strategies that are unforeseen and unknowable. Creating two sovereign capitals with defined and secure borders removes the factors of security and politics from Jerusalem and returns the problem of Jerusalem back to where it started—as a religious problem.

Combining sovereignty of two state capitals and international interests suggests placing the international zone boundaries on the inside. If the sole interest was the protection of the holy places, then there is no reason for a greater Jerusalem zone, a corpus separatum. An international Holy Basin zone would protect the Old City, Mount of Olives, and parts of Bethlehem, which are along the border of two unique cities, Jewish West Jerusalem and Palestinian East Jerusalem. This is very close to the current status quo and UN zones created after the 1948 war. This much smaller international Holy Basin upholds the primary purpose of security and access. A UN committee under UNSCOP suggested this concept of two capitals and an international zone, narrowed down to the Old City, and was support by the UN mission but rejected by the US State Department.[96] As an "impractical and undesirable" departure from the federal majority report supporting corpus separatum, this smaller Holy Basin "would severely limit the territorial area under the authority of the projected Governor of Jerusalem and thus weakening his authority and prestige as a guardian of the Holy Places throughout Palestine."[97]

There are issues with economic viability with the resulting Holy Basin population. A smaller zone is easier to control in terms of access and border crossings while ensuring the zone remains demilitarized. Limited space would

---

[96] UN Subcommittee 1 to the Ad Hoc Committee on the Palestinian Question, A/Ac 14/34, Ad Hoc Annex 19, 249.

[97] Yossi, *U.S. Policy on Jerusalem,* 11.

deny room for dozens of embassies; however, international legitimacy of two state capitals would result in a construction boom as embassies moved into both West and East Jerusalem districts. As was stated in section 1, not every holy place would be in this Holy Basin but would reflect the respective population's interests and other perspectives. To mitigate this discrepancy, the UN Holy Basin headquarters would be charged with coordinating security and access of all holy places and coordinating a joint archeological organization. The Sheikh Jarrah district north of the Old City, which contains portions of historic northern Old City walls, UNTSO offices, and national embassies, has been identified by President Obama as a conflict settlement that needs to be addressed when discussing an international Holy Basin methodology.[98]

There is risk in not asking follow-on questions or not diving down into specifics of what the two-state solution requires. Jerusalem has been generalized, glossed over, or ignored. On the other hand, researchers have come up with specific municipality solutions while ignoring religious and national interests from one or many sides. This negotiating process has taken sixty-three years just to return to a two-state solution, and it will continue to grow. Israel's animosity to the UN is causing them to ignore the danger of losing international legitimacy and sovereignty over East Jerusalem. Bilateral agreements between PNA and Israel ignore the fact that the international community will still deny sovereignty and international legitimacy to West Jerusalem. If East Jerusalem is declared the Palestinian capital, with the Green Line as the capital boundary, then Israel loses access to all its religious interests and may not even gain legitimacy over its own capital in bilateral talks. Israelis are not thinking past the status quo, and fighting for "One Jerusalem" will strip them of everything important.

Use of a Mandate to Internationalize the Jerusalem Holy Basin

Since Britain ended their League of Nations mandate in 1948, there had been eight wars between Israel and Arab nations. Since there is no standing United Nations force or a single nation ready to occupy and to provide security over Jerusalem, a UN-sponsored mandate concept could be used. A mandate concept accomplishes three objectives. It internationalizes the city, creates a secured environment for a new Palestinian state to create their institutions, and reflects the current security reality. If the international community grants Israel a mandate over the Holy Basin to maintain the status quo area for a period of

---

[98]   Steven Plaut, "Obama's Apartheid Plan for Jerusalem," *The Jewish Press*, 13 August 2009.

ten years, international benefits would follow without much change needed on the ground. This would allow the PNA to construct their state capital in East Jerusalem and provide time for other nations to adjust their embassy missions and locations to the new environment. The first ten years are required to set the conditions for a possible "joint" ten-year phase in Holy Basin management or a Palestinian-led mandate if the government progresses. There was an international city in a sense, before 1948, with Britain providing that outside mandate to protect the holy places. Before that, the Ottoman Empire provided the outside mandate that provided protection and access to religious sites. A UN-generated and temporary mandate is a method to internationalize the city without external troops while holding the mandate government accountable. The fear of a Palestinian-managed mandate would be a forcing function to convince Israel to accept the internationalization process.

An international Holy Basin zone methodology creates trust and accountability for each side, Hamas's 2006 Gaza elections created new understanding regarding bilateral negotiation tactics offered by the Palestinian Authority and future peace talks. Gaza residents were granted their desires, the removal of Jewish settlements and Israeli military forces, yet they still radicalized. Israelis cannot visualize a future state of Palestine where a Hamas terrorist who wishes to destroy Israel can move safely from Gaza to the West Bank to East Jerusalem and simply cross into the Israeli capital. Beirut showed that the religiously divided National Pact between groups created trust for a while but fell apart without external influences. Christians wanted trust from both sides to ensure they have access to their respective holy places. Israel's sovereignty resides on not just the Western Wall but the Temple Mount as well, with guaranteed access, security, and external legitimacy. Reality in Jerusalem has incrementally shifted to a close version of what each side desires. Even Ehud Barak stated, "There will be a special regime in place along with agreed upon arrangements in the Old City, the Mount of Olives and the City of David." The choices, risks, and operational methodologies are there for decision makers to act.

CONCLUSION AND PERSPECTIVES

In summary, this study argues that there are historical reasons to focus on Jerusalem first and to use an international Holy Basin methodology to bring Israel and the Palestinian National Authority together toward a workable compromise. This analysis identifies the strategic compromises required to create two distinct capital zones that grants sovereignty and legitimacy over respective capitals for the state of Israel and a future state of Palestine. The critical factors to achieve compromise are sovereignty over their respective capitals combined with international recognition for two capitals and possible control over remaining contested holy places.

Negotiations must be internationalized, not just bi-lateralized. The international community has perpetuated the conflict by withholding Jerusalem's sovereignty from Israel and from the Arab population. The UN continued to withhold sovereignty while the city was divided for nineteen years and again when the city was reunited in 1967. The Palestinian Authority cannot grant legitimacy to Israel's capital, and Israel has no reason to give away half of their capital when sixty-three years of hostility remains through years of UN resolutions withholding Jerusalem's sovereignty. Despite the more recent constructive tone between Israel and the PNA, the international community is required to help negotiations by providing focus, resources, and trust that provide opportunities for each side. Only the international community can reverse past corpus separatum ideas and grant sovereignty to both states over their respective capitals.

Within the two-state concept, sovereignty requirements over each state's capital as well as sovereignty over critical holy places have been overlooked. Two distinct cities in Jerusalem exist and may require some gerrymandering, but they do not follow the familiar 1949 armistice lines. These two capital zones must include sovereignty and legitimacy over key holy places critical to a nation's historical, religious, and nationalistic identity. The holy places define whether a negotiation agreement has internal legitimacy from their respective populations and outside stakeholders. Both President Abbas and Prime

Minister Netanyahu have stated that they would present an agreement to their citizens. While creating two distinct capital zones, workable methodologies must include the protection, supervision, and some level of sovereignty over key holy places. Unfortunately, the Old City, Temple Mount, and the Mount of Olives may forever remain contested.

Peace negotiations must recognize and incorporate the interests of both sides, but until Israelis and Palestinians are ready to strictly divide the Old City into two sections, an international Holy Basin zone can move Israelis and Palestinians incrementally from confrontation to cooperation. If the grand strategy is to get to where we want to go, then the distance between current reality and two sovereign states living side by side must be solved with compromise.[99] Each side has a vision of the future, and complex problems require a complex solution with support from the Quartet. A third international Holy Basin zone, limited in scope and created with a temporary international mandate, can create new emerging strategies that have the potential to bring both sides closer together.

Mark Twain, who visited Jerusalem in 1867, stated, "History doesn't repeat itself—at best it sometimes rhymes."[100] It has taken sixty-three years for Palestinians to come back to the two-state solution first approved by the United Nations; however, they continue to mix one-state ideas that assume Jews do not have any interest in Jerusalem. A two-state solution requires two sovereign capitals side by side with secure and defined boundaries. The lack of an international mandate while fighting for utopian concepts has perpetuated the conflict, delayed Palestinian self-determination, and has withheld sovereignty over Israeli's declared capital. Recognizing how close each side's proposals are, Alan Dershowitz noted that "the pragmatic new leaders of the Palestinian movement finally do want a Palestinian state more than they want the end of Israel."[101] In 1949, the little interest by the United States or any other nation to take the lead in Jerusalem resulted in a vacuum filled by war and conflict. A temporary mandate over the Holy Basin can be given to Israel and extended as needed. This closely reflects reality on the ground, internationalizes the city with accountability, and increases the time for Palestinians to develop their legitimate nation-state with professional institutions. A future environment that either divides the Old City and Temple Mount or bilateral management requires international approaches such as these to solve Jerusalem's complexity.

99 John Lewis Gaddis, "American Grand Strategy after War," speech prepared for the Karl Von Der Heyden Distinguished Lecture Series (Yale: Duke University, 26 February 2009).
100 Ibid.
101 Dershowitz, *Case for Peace*, 5.

Appendix A

Jerusalem Conflict Timeline

1916: Sykes-Picot Agreement annexing lands from the Ottoman Empire

1917: Balfour Declaration, Britain supports the creation of a Jewish State

1921: British Mandate over Palestine, codified in the League of Nations Charter

1937: Peel Commission recommending partition based on population centers

29 November 1947: The UN Partition Plan passed, UN General Assembly Resolution 181

1949: Armistice agreements created the Green Line separating West and East Jerusalem

9 December 1949: UNGA 303 supporting the internationalization of a large Jerusalem municipality, a corpus separatum, administered by the United Nations

5-11 June 1967: Six-Day War, unifying Jerusalem

22 November 1967: Approval of UNSCR 242

1968: PLO charter declared

6 October 1973: Yom Kippur War (or the Ramadan/October War)

1978: Camp David Egypt-Israeli peace talks with no discussion on Jerusalem

1980: UNSCR 476 ends occupation, including Jerusalem (assumes the entire city)

1982: First Lebanon War

October 1987: First intifada, surprising Arafat and the PLO

14 December 1988: Arafat's Declaration of Palestinian Independence, agreeing to the Israelis' right to exist

1990-1991 Persian Gulf War

December 1991: Madrid Conference where Israelis and PLO leadership met for the first time

September 1993: Oslo Accords, ending with the handshake of Rabin, Arafat, and Clinton

1994: Jerusalem Mayor Olmert closes the Arab Affairs office (created by Mayor Teddy Kollek)

May 1994: Arafat calls for jihad to liberate East Jerusalem

1995: Oslo II created five-year milestones; international community created the Palestinian Authority, granting levels of sovereignty over West Bank areas

October 1995: Beilin-Abu Mazen memorandum (first land swap proposal for 94-96 percent)

November 1995: PM Rabin assassinated at a peace rally

January 1997: Knesset creates bipartisan committee on Jerusalem

23 December 2000: Clinton proposes a Palestinian state based on 94-96 percent and 1-3 percent land swap

February 2001: Second intifada; election of Ariel Sharon as prime minister

2001: Israelis control the Orient House, Palestinian Authority headquarters in Jerusalem

2002: Arab initiative led by Saudi Arabia (Israel recognition based on the 1967 Green Line)

2002: UNSCR 1397 recognized the goal of two states with secure and recognized borders

30 April 2003: Road map issued by the Quartet

January 2006: Hamas wins election in Gaza (PNA PM Salam Fayyad)

July 2006: Second Lebanon War

May 2008: Gaza incursion, Operation Cast Lead

April 2009: Palestinian one-state conference held in Boston (biased)

14 June 2009: PM Netanyahu first publicly stated acceptance of two-state solution side by side at the Bar-Ilan University in Ramat Gan

30 June 2009: Start of six-month settlement freeze in East Jerusalem and the West Bank

September 2010: Latest peace process led by the Quartet

Appendix B

List of Abbreviations and Terms

ATFP	American Task Force for Palestine
EU	European Union
JIIS	Jerusalem Institute of Israeli Studies
JOCI	Jerusalem Old City Initiative
IPCRI	Israel/Palestinian Committee for Research and Information
Knesset	Israeli Parliament in West Jerusalem
NATO	North Atlantic Treaty Organization
NSS	National Security Strategy
OSCE	Organization for Security Cooperation in Europe

Quartet A temporary alliance of negotiators from the United Nations, United States, Russia, and the European Union

PLO	Palestinian Liberation Organization
PNA	Palestinian National Authority
Sharia	Religious courts
SFOR	NATO Stabilization Force for Bosnia (Dayton Peace Accords)
UN	United Nations

UNGA	United Nations General Assembly
UNSCR	United Nations Security Council Resolution
UNTSO	United Nations Truce Stabilization Organization
US	United States
Waqf	Muslim religious trust

BIBLIOGRAPHY

Primary Sources

Abbas, Mahmoud. Letter to Dr. Ziad Asali, President of American Task Force on Palestine. 13 October 2010.

Al-Mulhim, Abdulateef. "What if Arabs had recognized the State of Israel in 1948?" *Arab News*, 19 March 2011.

Balfour, Hugh. Letter to the US Secretary of State, Washington, DC, 13 January 1922, page 58, The Palestine mandate: The Division of Near Eastern Affairs, US Department of State, Salisbury, NC, 1977.

Beuvenisti, Meron. *Jerusalem: The Torn City*. Minneapolis: Israeli Typeset Limited, 1976.

Caradon, Lord Hugh Foot. *The Future of Jerusalem: A Review of Proposals for the Future of the City*. Washington, DC: National Defense University, 1979.

Clinton, Hillary. Speech at the American Task Force for Palestine fifth annual gala. Washington, DC, 20 October 2010.

Erakat, Saeb. *Erekat: We will seek UN Recognition Soon*. Ma'an News Agency. 21 March 2011.

Friedman, Thomas L. *From Beirut to Jerusalem*. New York: Anchor Books, 1989.

Glick, Caroline. Jerusalem Post Editor. Interview conducted on 19 January 2011.

Hanania, Ray. "A Peace Plan for All of Us." *Mideast Web*, 2 December 2009.

Segev, Yakir. Jerusalem Municipality Administrator for East Jerusalem. Interview conducted on 21 January 2011.

Shavit, Ari. "Barak: Israel ready to cede parts of Jerusalem in peace deal." *Haaretz*, 03 September 2010.

Wilson, Evan M. *Jerusalem, Key to Peace.* Washington, DC: The Middle East Institute, 1970.

"The Challenges of a One-State Solution," *Haaretz*, 20 June 2010.

Secondary Sources

Albin, Cecilia. "On the Future of Jerusalem. Under the title Negotiating Intractable Conflicts." *Cooperation and Conflict Journal 32.* (March 1997): 29-77.

American Task Force on Palestine. http://www.american task force on Palestine, 2011.

Aronson, Geoffrey. *Final Status Issues.* Jerusalem: Institute for Palestine Studies, 1996.

Auerback, Gedalia and Ira Sharkansky. *Politics and Planning in the Holy City.* New Brunswick: Transaction Publishers, 2007.

Avi-hai, Avraham. Ben-Gurion: State Builder Principles and Pragmatism 1948-1963. New York: Keter Publishing House, 1974.

Bar-Tal, Daniel. "Why Does Fear Override Hope in Societies Engulfed by Intractable Conflict, as it does in the Israeli Society?" *Political Psychology 22* (2010): 602.

Ben-Dov, Meir. *Carta's Illustrated History of Jerusalem, 2nd edition.* Jerusalem: Karta, 2006.

Boudreault, Jody, Naughton, Emma, Salaam, Yasser, eds. *US Official Statements: Israeli Settlements.* The Fourth Geneva Convention. Washington, DC: Institute for Palestine Studies, 1993.

Bovis, Eugene. *The Jerusalem Question: 1917-1968.* Stanford: Hoover Institution Press, 1971.

Breger, Marshall. *Jerusalem: A City and its Future.* Syracuse: Jerusalem Institute for Israel Studies, 2002.

Breger, Marshall, Yitzhak Reiter and Leonard Hammer. *Holy Places in the Israeli-Palestinian Conflict.* New York: Routledge, 2010.

Calame, Jon, Esther Charlesworth, and Lebbeus Woods. *Divided Cities: Belfast, Beirut, Jerusalem, Mostar and Nicosia.* 13 March 2009.

Caplan, Neal. *The Lausanne Conference, 1949, A Case Study in Middle East Peacemaking.* Occasional Papers 113. Tel Aviv University: The Moshe Dayan Center for Middle Eastern and African Studies, 1993.

Cheshin, Amir, Bill Hutman, and Avi Melawed. *Separate and Unequal: The Inside Story of Israeli Rule in East Jerusalem.* Cambridge, MA: Harvard University Press, 1999.

Dershowitz, Alan. *The Case for Israel.* Hoboken, NJ: John Wiley and Sons, 2003.

Dumper, Michael. *The Politics of Sacred Space: The Old City of Jerusalem in the Middle East Conflict.* Boulder, CO: Lynne Reiner Publishers, 2002.

Dumper, Michael. *The Politics of Jerusalem Since 1967.* New York: Columbia University Press, 1997.

Emmett, Chad F. "The Status Quo Solution for Jerusalem." *Journal of Palestinian Studies 26* (Winter, 1997): 16-28.

Englard, Itzhak. *The Status of the Holy Places in Jerusalem.* Ahimeir: Jerusalem Papers on Peace, 2007.

Feintuch, Yossi. *US Policy on Jerusalem: Contributions in Political Science.* Report no. 191. New York: Greenwood Press, 1987.

Ferrari, Silvio. "The Holy See and the postwar Palestine issue: the internationalization of Jerusalem and the protection of the Holy Places," *International Affairs*, 261.

Fukuyama, Francis. *State-Building.* Ithaca, New York: Cornell University Press, 2004.

Gaddis, John Lewis. "American Grand Strategy after War." Speech prepared for the Karl Von Der Heyden Distinguished Lecture. Yale: Duke University, 26 February 2009.

Gold, Dore. *Jerusalem Final Status.* Tel Aviv: Jaffee Center for Strategic Studies, 1995.

Gold, Dore. *The Fight for Jerusalem.* Washington, DC: Dore Gold Books, 2007.

Hill, Charles. *Grand Strategies.* New Haven: Yale University Press, 2010.

Holbrook, Richard. *To End a War.* New York: The Modern Library, 1999.

Hulme, David. "Identity, Ideology and the Future of Jerusalem." *Vision.org*, 2006.

Ibish, Hussein. *What's Wrong with the One-State Solution.* Washington, DC: American Task Force on Palestine, 2009.

Ingram, O. Kelly ed. *Jerusalem: Key to Peace in the Middle East.* Durham, NC: Triangle Friends of the Middle East, 1978.

Jaffee Center for Strategic Studies Study Group. *The West Bank and Gaza: Israel's Options for Peace.* Tel Aviv: JCSS, 1989.

Kairos Document. "A Moment of Truth." December 2009. http://www.kairospalestine.ps.

Klein, Menachem. *The Jerusalem Problem: A Review of Forty Years of Israeli Rule over Arab Jerusalem. Israel Studies* 13 (Summer 2008).

Marcus, Amy. Jerusalem 1913: *The Origins of the Arab-Israel Conflict.* New York: Viking Penguin Group, 2007.

Matthews, Charles D. "A Muslim Iconoclast on the Merits of Jerusalem and Palestine," *Journal of the American Oriental Society* 56 (March 1936).

Newsweek. "The One State Solution." 20 September 2008.

Oesterreicher, John M. *Internationalization of Jerusalem*. South Orange NJ: Seton Hall University Press, 1971.

Pfaff, Richard H. *Jerusalem: Keystone of an Arab-Israeli Settlement*. Washington, DC: American Enterprise Institute, 1969.

Qupty, Mazen. *The Legal Framework for a Special Regime: The Old City of Jerusalem*. University of Windsor, Ontario, Canada: 2010.

Ramon, Amnon. *The Historic Basin: Problems and Possible Solutions*. Jerusalem Institute for Israeli Studies. Jerusalem, 2007.

Reiter, Yitzhak. *Options for the Administration of the Holy Places in the Old City of Jerusalem*. Jerusalem: Jerusalem Institute for Israeli Studies, 2008.

Romann, Michael and Alex Weingrod. *Living Together Separately: Arabs and Jews in contemporary Jerusalem*. Princeton: Princeton University Press, 1991.

Segal, Jerome M., Levy Shlomit, Nadar Izzat Sa'id, Elihu Katz. *Negotiating Jerusalem*. Albany, NY: State University of New York Press, 2000.

Schmid, Dorothee. "Mapping European and American Economic Initiatives towards Israel and the Palestinian Authority and their Effects on Honest Broker Perceptions." *EuroMESCO 61* (October 2006).

Sharon, Aryeh. *Planning Jerusalem: The Master Plan for the Old city of Jerusalem and its Environs*. New York: McGraw-Hill, 1974.

Shepard, Jones S. "The Legal Status of Jerusalem: Some National and International Aspects." *Law and Contemporary Problems 33* (Winter 1968).

Simpson, Steven. "Islam will never accept Jewish State." *American Thinker*, 30 Jun 2010.

Terence Prittie, *Whose Jerusalem?*. London: Frederick Miller Limited, 1981.

The Palestinian Academic Society for the Study of International Affairs. *Jerusalem Municipal Boundaries: 1947-2000*. http://www.passia.org.

The Palestine Mandate. Salisbury, NC: US Department of State Division of Near Eastern Affairs, 1977.

Thomson, Janice E. Mercenaries. *Pirates, and Sovereigns: State-Building and Extraterritorial Violence in Early Modern Europe*. Princeton: Princeton University Press, 1994.

Time Magazine. "Israel: Unifying a Divided City." 20 November 1978.

Truax, Patrick. "A New Tack in the Holy Land." *Digital Journal*. 29 December 2008. http://www.digitaljournal.com/article/.

Vaughn, Andrew G. and Ann E. Killebrew. *Jerusalem in Bible and Archaeology: the First Temple Period*. Atlanta: The Society of Biblical Literature, 2003.

Wasserstein, Bernard. *Divided Jerusalem*, 3rd ed. New Haven: Yale University Press, 2008.

Weber, Max. *Politics as a Vocation*. H.H. Gerth and C. Wright Mils, eds. New York: Oxford University Press, 1958.

United Nations General Assembly Resolution 181, 29 November 1947. http://un.org/documents/sc/res.

United Nations Security Council Resolution 50, 1948.

United Nations Security Council Resolution 242, 22 November 1967.

UN Sub-Committee 1 to the Ad Hoc Committee on the Palestinian Question, A/Ac 14/34, Ad Hoc Annex 19.

United Nations Trust Supervision Organization. http://wwwupdate.un.org/en/peacekeeping/missions/untso/.

Index

www.ingramcontent.com/pod-product-compliance
Lightning Source LLC
Chambersburg PA
CBHW021244280526
45784CB00005B/2232